MORE JUNIOR HIGH • MIDDLE SCHOOL

TALKSHEETS

—Updated!

50
CREATIVE DISCUSSIONS FOR
JUNIOR HIGH YOUTH GROUPS

DAVID LYNN

ZONDERVAN™

GRAND RAPIDS, MICHIGAN 49530

More Junior High–Middle School TalkSheets—Updated! 50 creative discussions for junior high youth groups

Copyright © 2001 by Youth Specialties

Youth Specialties books, 300 S. Pierce St., El Cajon, CA 92020, are published by Zondervan, 5300 Patterson Ave. S.E., Grand Rapids, MI 49530

Library of Congress Cataloging-in-Publication Data

Lynn, David, 1954-
    More junior high/middle school talksheets — updated! : 50 creative discussion starters for youth groups / David Lynn.
        p. cm. — (TalkSheets series)
        ISBN 0-310-23856-0
        1. Church group work with teenagers. 2. Junior high school students—Religious life. 3. Middle school students—Religious life. I. Title. II. Series.

BV4447 .L9612 2001
286'.433—dc21

00-043940

Web site addresses listed in this book were current at the time of publication, but we can't guarantee they're still operational. If you have trouble with an URL, please contact us via e-mail (YS@YouthSpecialties.com) to let us know if you've found the correct or new URL or if the URL is no longer operational.

Edited by Mary Fletcher, Anita Palmer, and Tamara Rice
Interior and cover design by PAZ Design Group
Illustrations and borders by Rick Sealock

Printed in the United States of America

    02 03 04 05 06 07 /VG/ 10 9 8 7 6 5 4

CONTENTS

MORE JUNIOR HIGH • MIDDLE SCHOOL

TALKSHEETS

—Updated!

THE HOWS AND WHATS OF TALKSHEETS

You are holding a very valuable book! No, it won't make you a genius or millionaire. But it does contain 50 instant discussions for junior high and middle school kids. Inside you'll find reproducible TalkSheets that cover a variety of hot topics—plus simple, step-by-step instructions on how to use them. All you need is this book, a few copies of the handouts, and some kids (and maybe a snack or two). You're on your way to landing on some serious issues in kids' lives today.

These TalkSheets are user-friendly and very flexible. They can be used in a youth group meeting, a Sunday school class, or in a Bible study group. You can adapt them for either large or small groups. And, they can be covered in only 20 minutes or explored more intensively in two hours.

You can build an entire youth group meeting around a single TalkSheet, or you can use TalkSheets to supplement other materials and resources you might be using. These are tools for you—how you use them is your choice.

More Junior High–Middle School TalkSheets—Updated! is not your average curriculum or workbook. This collection of discussions will get your kids involved and excited about talking through important issues. The TalkSheets deal with key topics and include interesting activities, challenging questions, and eye-catching graphics. They will challenge your kids to think about opinions, learn about themselves, and grow in their faith.

LEADING A TALKSHEET DISCUSSION

TalkSheets can be used as a curriculum for your youth group, but they are designed to be springboards for discussion. They encourage your kids to take part and interact with each other while talking about real life issues. And hopefully they'll do some serious thinking,

discover new ideas for themselves, defend their points of view, and make decisions.

Youth today face a world of moral confusion. Youth leaders must teach the church's beliefs and values—and also help young people make the right choices in a world with so many options. Teenagers are bombarded with the voices of society and media messages—most of which drown out what they hear from the church.

A TalkSheet discussion works for this very reason. While dealing with the questions and activities on the TalkSheet, your kids will think carefully about issues, compare their beliefs and values with others, and make their own choices. TalkSheets will challenge your group to explain and rework their ideas in a Christian atmosphere of acceptance, support, and growth.

The most common fear of junior high and middle school youth group leaders is, "What will I do if the kids in my group just sit there and don't say anything?" Well, when kids don't have anything to say, it's because they haven't had a chance or time to get their thoughts organized! Most young people haven't developed the ability to think on their feet. Since many are afraid they might sound stupid, they don't know how to voice their ideas and opinions.

The solution? TalkSheets let your kids deal with the issues in a challenging, non-threatening way before the actual discussion begins. They'll have time to organize their thoughts, write them down, and ease their fears about participating. They may even look forward to sharing their answers! Most importantly, they'll (most likely) want to find out what others said and open up to talk through the topics.

If you're still a little leery about the success of a real discussion among your kids, that's okay! The only way to get them rolling is to get them started.

YOUR ROLE AS THE LEADER

The best discussions don't happen by accident. They require careful preparation and a sensitive leader. Don't worry if you aren't experienced or don't have hours to prepare.

TalkSheets are designed to help even the novice leader! The more TalkSheet discussions you lead, the easier it becomes. Keep the following tips in mind when using the TalkSheets as you get your kids talking.

BE CHOOSY

Each TalkSheet deals with a different topic. Choose a TalkSheet based on the needs and the maturity level of your group. Don't feel obligated to use the TalkSheets in the order they appear in this book. Use your best judgment and mix them up however you want—they are tools for you!

TRY IT YOURSELF

Once you have chosen a TalkSheet for your group, answer the questions and do the activities yourself. Imagine your kids' reactions to the TalkSheet. This will help you prepare for the discussion and understand what you are asking them to do. Plus, you'll have some time to think of other appropriate questions, activities, and Bible verses.

GET SOME INSIGHT

On each leader's guide page, you'll find numerous tips and ideas for getting the most out of your discussion. You may want to add some of your own thoughts or ideas in the margins. And, there's room to keep track of the date and the name of your group at the top of the leader's page. You'll also find suggestions for additional activities and discussion questions.

There are some references to Internet links throughout the TalkSheets. These are guides for you to find the resources and information that you need. For additional help, be sure to visit the Youth Specialties Web site at www.YouthSpecialties.com for information on materials and further links to finding what you need.

MAKE COPIES

Kids will need their own copy of the TalkSheet. Only make copies of the student's side of the TalkSheet! The material on the reverse side (the leader's guide) is just for you. You're able to make copies for your group because we've given you permission to do so. U.S. copyright laws have not changed, and it is still mandatory to request permission from a publisher before making copies of other published material. It is against the law not to do so. However, permission is given for you to make copies of this material for your group only, not for every youth group in your state. Thank you for cooperating.

INTRODUCE THE TOPIC

It's important to introduce the topic before you pass out the TalkSheets to your group. Depending on your group, keep it short and to the point. Be careful not to over-introduce the topic, sound preachy, or resolve the issue before you've started. Your goal is to spark their interest and leave plenty of room for discussion.

The best way to do this is verbally. You can tell a story, share an experience, or describe a situation or problem having to do with the topic. You might want to jump-start your group by asking something like, "What is the first thing you think of when you hear the word _____ [insert the topic]?" Then, after a few answers have been given, you can add something like, "Well, it seems we all have different ideas about this subject. Tonight we're going to investigate it a bit further..." Then pass out the TalkSheet and be sure that everyone has a pencil or pen. Now you're on your way! The following are excellent methods you can use to introduce any topic in this book—

- Show a related short film or video.
- Read a passage from a book or magazine that relates to the subject.
- Play a popular CD that deals with the topic.
- Perform a short skit or dramatic presentation.
- Play a simulation game or role-play, setting up the topic.
- Present current statistics, survey results, or read a current newspaper article that provides recent information about the topic.
- Use an icebreaker or other crowd game, getting into the topic in a humorous way. For example if the topic is fun, play a game to begin the discussion. If the topic is success, consider a

game that helps the kids experience success or failure.

- Use posters, videos, or any other visuals to help focus attention on the topic.

There are endless possibilities for an intro—you are limited only by your own creativity! Each TalkSheet offers a few suggestions, but you are free to use any method with which you feel most comfortable. But do keep in mind that the introduction is a very important part of each session.

SET BOUNDARIES

It'll be helpful to set a few ground rules before the discussion. Keep the rules to a minimum, of course, but let the kids know what's expected of them. Here are suggestions for some basic ground rules—

- **What is said in this room stays in this room.** Emphasize the importance of confidentiality. Some kids will open up, some won't. Confidentiality is vital for a good discussion. If your kids can't keep the discussion in the room, then they won't open up.
- **No put-downs.** Mutual respect is important. If your kids disagree with some opinions, ask them to comment on the subject (but not on the other person). It's okay to attack the ideas, but not other people.
- **There is no such thing as a dumb question.** Your group members must feel free to ask questions at any time. The best way to learn is to ask questions and get answers.
- **No one is forced to talk.** Let everyone know they have the right to pass or not answer any question.
- **Only one person speaks at a time.** This is a mutual respect issue. Everyone's opinion is worthwhile and deserves to be heard.

Communicate with your group that everyone needs to respect these boundaries. If you sense that your group members are attacking each other or getting a negative attitude during the discussion, do stop and deal with the problem before going on.

ALLOW ENOUGH TIME

Pass out copies of the TalkSheet to your kids after the introduction and make sure that each person has a pen or pencil and a Bible. There are usually five or six activities on each TalkSheet. If your time

is limited, or if you are using only a part of the TalkSheet, tell the group to complete only the activities you'd like them to.

Decide ahead of time whether or not you would like the kids to work on the TalkSheets individually or in groups.

Let them know how much time they have for completing the TalkSheet and let them know when there is a minute (or so) left. Go ahead and give them some extra time and then start the discussion when everyone seems ready to go.

SET THE STAGE

Create a climate of acceptance. Most teenagers are afraid to voice their opinions because they don't want to be laughed at or look stupid in front of their peers. They want to feel safe if they're going to share their feelings and beliefs. Communicate that they can share their thoughts and ideas—even if they may be different or unpopular. If your kids get put-downs, criticism, laughter, or snide comments (even if their statements are opposed to the teachings of the Bible) it'll hurt the discussion.

Always phrase your questions—even those that are printed on the TalkSheets—so that you are asking for an opinion, not an answer. For example if a question reads, "What should Bill have done in that situation?" change it to, "What do you think Bill should have done in that situation?" The simple addition of the three words "do you think" makes the question less threatening and a matter of opinion, rather than a demand for the right answer. Your kids will relax when they will feel more comfortable and confident. Plus, they'll know that you actually care about their opinions and they'll feel appreciated!

LEAD THE DISCUSSION

Discuss the TalkSheet with the group and encourage all your kids to participate. Communicate that it's important for them to respect each other's opinions and feelings! The more they contribute, the better the discussion will be.

If your youth group is big, you may divide it into smaller groups of six to 12. Each of these small groups should have a facilitator—either an adult leader or a student member—to keep the discussion going. Remind the facilitators not to dominate the others. If the group looks to the facilitator for an answer, ask him or her to direct the questions or responses back to the group. Once the smaller groups have completed their discussions, combine them into one large group and ask the different groups to share their ideas.

You don't have to divide the groups up with every TalkSheet. For some discussions, you may want to vary the group size and or divide the meeting into groups of the same sex.

The discussion should target the questions and answers on the TalkSheet. Go through them one at a time and ask the kids to share their responses. Have them compare their answers and brainstorm new ones in addition to the ones they've written down. Encourage them to share their opinions and answers, but don't force those who are quiet.

AFFIRM ALL RESPONSES—RIGHT OR WRONG

Let your kids know that their comments and contributions are appreciated and important. This is especially true for those who rarely speak up in group activities. Make a point of thanking them for joining in. This will be an incentive for them to participate further.

Remember that affirmation doesn't mean approval. Affirm even those comments that seem wrong to you. You'll show that everyone has a right to express their ideas—no matter how controversial they may be. If someone states an opinion that is off base, make a mental note of the comment. Then in your wrap-up, come back to the comment or present a different point of view in a positive way. But don't reprimand the student who voiced the comment.

DON'T BE THE AUTHORITATIVE ANSWER

Some kids think you have the right answer to every question. They'll look to you for approval, even when they are answering another group member's question. If they start to focus on you for answers, redirect them toward the group by making a comment like, "Remember that you're talking to everyone, not just me."

Your goal as the facilitator is to keep the discussion alive and kicking. It's important that your kids think of you as a member of the group—on their level. The less authoritative you are, the

more value your own opinions will have. If your kids view you as a peer, they will listen to your comments. You have a tremendous responsibility to be, with sincerity, their trusted friend.

LISTEN TO EACH PERSON

God gave you one mouth and two ears. Good discussion leaders know how to listen. Although it's tempting at times, don't monopolize the discussion. Encourage others to talk first— then express your opinions during your wrap up.

DON'T FORCE IT

Encourage all your kids to talk, but don't make them comment. Each member has the right to pass. If you feel that the discussion isn't going well, go on to the next question or restate the question to keep them moving.

DON'T TAKE SIDES

You'll probably have different opinions expressed in the group from time to time. Be extra careful not to take one side or another. Encourage both sides to think through their positions—ask questions to get them deeper. If everyone agrees on an issue, you can play devil's advocate with tough questions and stretch their thinking. Remain neutral—your point of view is your own, not that of the group.

DON'T LET ANYONE (INCLUDING YOU) TAKE OVER

Nearly every youth group has one person who likes to talk and is perfectly willing to express an opinion on any subject. Try to encourage equal participation from all the kids.

SET UP FOR THE TALK

Make sure that the seating arrangement is inclusive and encourages a comfortable, safe atmosphere for discussion. Theater-style seating (in rows) isn't discussion-friendly. Instead, arrange the chairs in a circle or semicircle (or on the floor with pillows!).

LET THEM LAUGH!

Discussions can be fun! Most of the TalkSheets include questions that'll make them laugh and get them thinking, too.

LET THEM BE SILENT

Silence can be a scary for discussion leaders! Some react by trying to fill the silence with a question or a comment. The following suggestions may help you to handle silence more effectively—

- Be comfortable with silence. Wait it out for 30 seconds or so to respond. You may want to restate the question to give your kids a gentle nudge.
- Talk about the silence with the group. What does the silence mean? Do they really not have any comments? Maybe they're confused, embarrassed, or don't want to share.
- Answer the silence with questions or comments like, "I know this is challenging to think about..." or "It's scary to be the first to talk." If you acknowledge the silence, it may break the ice.
- Ask a different question that may be easier to handle or that will clarify the one already posed. But don't do this too quickly without giving them time to think the first one through.

KEEP IT UNDER CONTROL

Monitor the discussion. Be aware if the discussion is going in a certain direction or off track. This can happen fast, especially if the kids disagree or things get heated. Mediate wisely and set the tone that you want. If your group gets bored with an issue, get them back on track. Let the discussion unfold, but be sensitive to your group and who is or is not getting involved.

If a student brings up a side issue that's interesting, decide whether or not to purse it. If discussion is going well and the issue is worth discussion, let them talk it through. But, if things get way off track, say something like, "Let's come back to that subject later if we have time. Right now, let's finish our discussion on..."

BE CREATIVE AND FLEXIBLE

You don't have to follow the order of the questions on the TalkSheet. Follow your own creative instinct. If you find other ways to use the TalkSheets, use them! Go ahead and add other questions or Bible references.

Don't feel pressured to spend time on every single activity. If you're short on time, you can skip some items. Stick with the questions that are the most interesting to the group.

SET YOUR GOALS

TalkSheets are designed to move along toward a goal, but you need to identify your goal in advance. What would you like your young people to learn? What truth should they discover? What is the goal of the session? If you don't know where you're going, it's doubtful you will get there.

BE THERE FOR YOUR KIDS

Some kids may want to talk more with you (you got 'em thinking!). Let them know that you can talk one-on-one with them afterwards.

Communicate to the kids that they can feel free to talk with you about anything with confidentiality. Let them know you're there for them with support and concern, even after the TalkSheet discussion has been completed.

USE THE BIBLE

Most adults believe the Bible has authority over their lives. It's common for adults to start their discussions or to support their arguments with Bible verses. But today's teenagers form their opinions and beliefs from their own life situations first—then they decide how the Bible fits their needs. TalkSheets start with the realities of the adolescent world and then move toward the Bible. You'll be able to show them that the Bible can be their guide and that God does have something to say to them about their own unique situations.

The last activity on each TalkSheet uses Bible verses that were chosen for their application to each issue. But they aren't exhaustive. Feel free to add whatever other verses you think would fit well and add to the discussion.

After your kids read the verses, ask them to think how the verses apply to their lives and summarize the meanings for them.

For example, after reading the passages for "Buy Now, Pay Later," you may summarize by saying something like, "God wants us to be responsible with our money. It's easy to let greed get in the way of putting God first. God gives us what we need—all the time."

CLOSE THE DISCUSSION

Present a challenge to the group by asking yourself, "What do I want the kids to remember most from this discussion?" There's your wrap-up! It's important to conclude by affirming the group and offering a summary that ties the discussion together.

Sometimes you won't need a wrap-up. You may want to leave the issue hanging and discuss it in another meeting. That way, your group can think about it more and you can nail down the final ideas later.

TAKE IT FURTHER

On the leader's guide page, you'll find additional discussion activities—labeled More—for following up on the discussion. These aren't a must, but highly recommended. They let the kids reflect upon, evaluate, review, and assimilate what they've learned. These activities may lead to more discussion and better learning.

After you've done the activity, be sure to debrief your kids on the activity, either now or at the next group meeting. A few good questions to ask about the activity are—

* What happened when you did this activity or discussion?

* Was it helpful or a waste of time?

* How did you feel when doing the activity or discussion?

* Did the activity/discussion make you think differently or affect you in any way?

* In one sentence state what you learned from this activity or discussion.

A FINAL WORD TO THE WISE — THAT'S YOU!

Some of these TalkSheets deal with topics that may be sensitive or controversial for your kids. Issues like sexuality or materialism aren't discussed openly in some churches. You're encouraging discussion and inviting your kids to express their opinions. As a result, you may be criticized by parents or others in your church who may not see the importance of such discussions. Use your best judgment. If you suspect that a particular TalkSheet will cause problems, you may not want to use it. Or you may want to tweak a particular TalkSheet and only cover some of the questions. Either way, the potential bad could outweigh the good—better safe than sorry. To avoid any misunderstanding, you may want to give the parents or senior pastor (or whoever else you are accountable to) copies of the TalkSheet before you use it. Let them know the discussion you would like to have and the goal you are hoping to accomplish. Challenge your kids to take their TalkSheet home to talk about it with their parents. How would their parents, as young people, have answered the questions? Your kids may find that their parents understand them better than they thought! Also, encourage them to think of other Bible verses or ways that the TalkSheet applies to their lives.

THE NEXT STEP

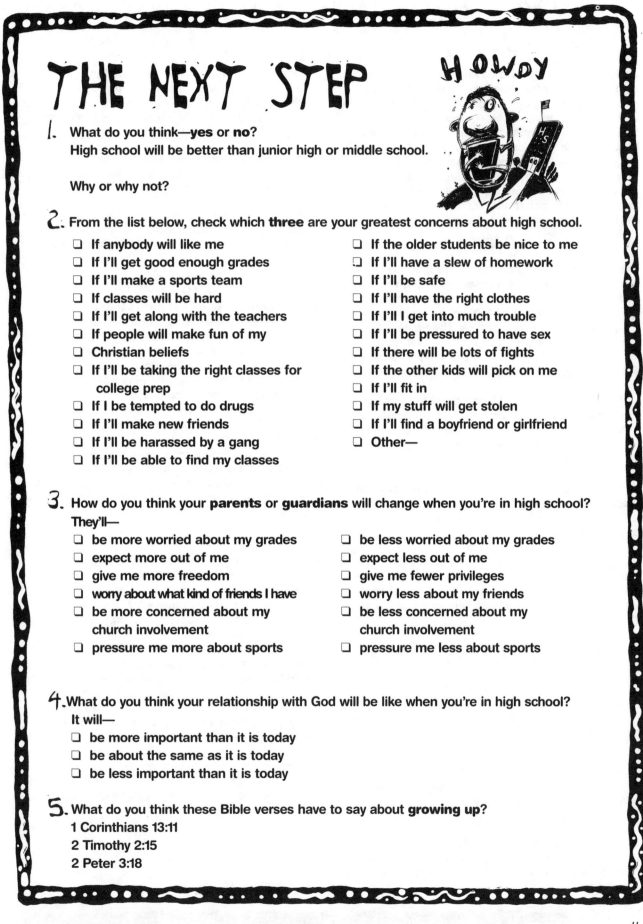

HOWDY

1. What do you think—**yes** or **no**?
High school will be better than junior high or middle school.

Why or why not?

2. From the list below, check which **three** are your greatest concerns about high school.

- ❑ If anybody will like me
- ❑ If I'll get good enough grades
- ❑ If I'll make a sports team
- ❑ If classes will be hard
- ❑ If I'll get along with the teachers
- ❑ If people will make fun of my
- ❑ Christian beliefs
- ❑ If I'll be taking the right classes for college prep
- ❑ If I be tempted to do drugs
- ❑ If I'll make new friends
- ❑ If I'll be harassed by a gang
- ❑ If I'll be able to find my classes

- ❑ If the older students be nice to me
- ❑ If I'll have a slew of homework
- ❑ If I'll be safe
- ❑ If I'll have the right clothes
- ❑ If I'll I get into much trouble
- ❑ If I'll be pressured to have sex
- ❑ If there will be lots of fights
- ❑ If the other kids will pick on me
- ❑ If I'll fit in
- ❑ If my stuff will get stolen
- ❑ If I'll find a boyfriend or girlfriend
- ❑ Other—

3. How do you think your **parents** or **guardians** will change when you're in high school? They'll—

- ❑ be more worried about my grades
- ❑ expect more out of me
- ❑ give me more freedom
- ❑ worry about what kind of friends I have
- ❑ be more concerned about my church involvement
- ❑ pressure me more about sports

- ❑ be less worried about my grades
- ❑ expect less out of me
- ❑ give me fewer privileges
- ❑ worry less about my friends
- ❑ be less concerned about my church involvement
- ❑ pressure me less about sports

4. What do you think your relationship with God will be like when you're in high school? It will—
- ❑ be more important than it is today
- ❑ be about the same as it is today
- ❑ be less important than it is today

5. What do you think these Bible verses have to say about **growing up**?
1 Corinthians 13:11
2 Timothy 2:15
2 Peter 3:18

THE NEXT STEP [transitioning into high school]

THIS WEEK

Junior highers or middle schoolers in transition to high school are often filled with both anticipation and dread. Moving up to high school often begins in a panic. Some teens interpret change as loss—they lose familiarity with the old school structure, relationships with teachers and friends, or involvement in sports and other extracurricular activities. Christian young people often worry about how others will respond to their faith. This TalkSheet will give them a chance to talk about their apprehensions and cope with the transition.

OPENER

What are your kids' fears about the first day of high school? You might be surprised what they're thinking about! You may want to have your group make up a "plot by plot" story. Start the plot by saying something like the following phrases. Then have another person add the next part of the plot. And then someone else can add the next part of the plot until the story is done! Starters include phrases like this—

- It was the first day of high school for Luis, who...
- Samantha was walking into cafeteria when...
- After looking for her best friend, Anna decided to...
- As Seth strolled to his first class...
- Bryce was nervous because he'd just seen...

Your group may end up with a wild introduction to a discussion on what high school might be like. But, be sure they keep it clean and focused on the first day of high school.

You can play this the same way by using a large piece of white paper or a white board to write on. Either you or one of your kids writes the initial sentence up on the paper or white board and then the others can take turns adding sentences to the story. Continue until the story is finished.

THE DISCUSSION, BY NUMBERS

1. Ask for volunteers to some of their responses and why. You may want to share some of the feelings you had when you were their age. Listen carefully—you'll learn a lot about how they're feeling!

2. You may want to give the group members a chance to identify their top five questions, then compile a group top 10 list as they place their votes. When you are finished, you might want to answer the top 10 questions together as a group.

3. Kids in transition want freedom and security—they want to move away from their parents, but still hope their parents will still be there for them. Don't let this turn into a gripe session about parents, but instead look at what would be reasonable changes for parents to make and why. This is an opportunity for you to empathize with kids and support parental authority.

4. As students share their answers, explore why or why not their relationship with God might change. How will the relationship change?

5. Ask the students to relate these passages to the move to high school. Point out that God is there for them as they go through the changes in their lives.

THE CLOSE

As you summarize the key points that have been made during the discussion, make it clear that their fears and apprehensions are normal. They're facing new challenges, struggles, and adventures—some they can control and some they can't. You (or another leader in your group) may want to share a story about your transition to high school. Encourage them to look at the changes as new opportunities to meet others, try new activities, and learn about themselves.

Finally, you may want to wrap up by reading Psalm 20 (or another psalm) that deals with trust and security in God. Take some time to pray for the group and for those who are feeling nervous about the future.

MORE

- How does TV portray the move to high school? Ask the group to think of situations in movies or on TV that show this transition. You may want to show clips of a few of these TV shows (check out the prime time line-ups). What happened in the stories? What were the problems that occurred and how were they handled? How do these shows or movies make your kids feel about high school?

- What questions about high school do your middle schoolers have? Try a Q&A session with some of your older high school students! Ask your junior highers to (anonymously) write down questions about high school on 3x5 cards—or have your junior highers or middle schoolers to write short, anonymous letters to high school students, expressing their concerns about high school. Then collect them and hand them off to the high school panel to answer.

SEXUAL STUFF

1. How often do you and your friends talk about **sexual stuff**?

   ❑ A lot—every time we hang out.
   ❑ Often—but only with my closest friends.
   ❑ Sometimes—if something comes up.
   ❑ Hardly ever—my friends don't talk about it much.

2. Where do most people your age get information about sex? Check the **top three.**

   ❑ Bible
   ❑ Magazines or books
   ❑ Youth group leaders
   ❑ Friends
   ❑ Internet
   ❑ Teachers
   ❑ Movies
   ❑ Sex ed classes
   ❑ Parents or guardians
   ❑ Television
   ❑ Pastor or youth pastor
   ❑ Family planning clinics
   ❑ Other—

3. Put an **arrow** ⇨ by the one that's true for you—

   I've talked about sex with at least one of my parents.
   I've talked about sex with both of my parents.
   I haven't talked about sex with either of my parents.

4. What does your **church** believe about sex? Have you learned anything about sex in church?

5. Circle the **top five** things you'd want students to learn if you were teaching a sex education class at your school.

   What God has to say about sex
   Relationships
   Reasons to wait until marriage
   How to have sex
   Sexually transmitted diseases
   Internet pornography
   Birth control
   Abortion
   What adults think about sex
   Sexual abuse

   Pregnancy
   Sexual differences between males and females
   What girls and boys each think about sex
   Homosexuality
   Sexual morals
   How to say no
   Bodily changes
   The good stuff about sex
   Sex in the media

6. Check out **Proverbs 7:1-27**—in your own words, how do you think it applies to sex education?

SEXUAL STUFF [sex education]

THIS WEEK

Sex education—information about sex—is part of most junior high and middle school curriculum. Young teenagers are constantly bombarded with messages that premarital sex is acceptable—and normal. This TalkSheet offers the opportunity to talk with young people about the kind of sex education they've had and what they need to know.

OPENER

Whatever you do for your intro, communicate that sex is a normal, healthy part of a loving, committed relationship. Our society has warped its meaning—that's why you're going to talk about it!

Start by asking them why they think God created sex. What have your kids been told about sex in the church? Read in the Bible? Make a list of their ideas on a poster board or whiteboard. Then ask the group to list where sex is shown, talked about, referred to, and sung about in the media. Keep a separate list of these on a poster or whiteboard. How was sexual activity portrayed? Was it good? Bad? Dirty? Uncomfortable? How has the media warped the meaning of sex?

Communicate that this discussion is not intended to condemn or put blame on anyone. If any of your kids don't want to share, that's okay. Encourage them to respect each other's thoughts and especially to keep whatever is shared among the group confidential.

THE DISCUSSION, BY NUMBERS

1. Point out that puberty and natural curiosity encourage an interest in sex—which is normal and healthy, not sinful! God created the hormones in people's bodies that get them thinking about sex. It isn't their interest in sex that is sinful—it's the decisions they make as a result of that interest that get them into trouble!

2. Inventory the group's top three or four choices. Which source on the list would be the most dependable? Which is most helpful? Most of the info they get is misleading and they absorb it without even knowing it.

3. Why is it difficult for your kids to talk to their parents about sex? How many of them have talked with the adults in their lives? At what age? What did their parents say about sex?

4. It would be a good idea to write down what the church believes—then discuss with your group which are true and which are false. How do these compare with what the world believes about sex?

5. What parts of sex education do your students think is important? Why or why not? What would they like to know more about?

6. What do these verses say about sex ed? Point out that God wants the best for all of us, which is why he reserved sex for marriage.

THE CLOSE

Summarize the points that have been covered, but focus on God's forgiveness. Some of your kids may already have done things they regret and feel guilty about. You may wish to read Isaiah 1:18 or 1 John 1:9 about God's forgiveness and compassion—God forgives and forgets—it's never too late to start over.

Emphasize your willingness to talk to them about sexual topics they may need to discuss privately and confidentially. If they'd like more information about sex, encourage them to talk with their parents or guardians. You may want to suggest a few books that address sex from a Christian perspective. See also Too Much Too Soon (page 73). Or you may want to end with a challenge to commit to abstinence. For more information, check out Aim for Success (www.aim-for-success.org), True Love Waits (www.truelovewaits.com), or the Youth Specialties Web page (www.YouthSpecialties.com) for links to information and resources.

Close with a time of prayer, asking God for his strength and wisdom with sexual choices. Give your kids a time of silent prayer and challenge them to bring their struggles, hurts, or regrets to God.

MORE

● Some of your kids may have dealt with rape, sexual abuse, or abortion. Under no circumstances should anyone sexually abuse or rape another person. Both rape and sexual abuse are crimes, punished by years in prison (or worse). If your kids are victims of sexual aggression—or suspect others are—they must get help immediately from a school counselor, parent, pastor, or you. For more information, visit the Rape, Abuse, and Incest National Network (www.rainn.org) or National Coalition Against Sexual Assault (http://ncasa.org).

● What statements could be used to pressure someone into having premarital sex (i.e. "everyone else is")? Make a list of your group's ideas. How would your kids respond to these lines? You may want to role play these situations to see how your kids would respond.

MORE THAN FRIENDS

1. **What's your opinion?**
   The best age for a girl to start going out with guys is—

   The best age for a guy to start going out with girls is—

2. How much **pressure** is there at your school to have a boyfriend or girlfriend?
   - ❑ A lot of pressure
   - ❑ Some pressure
   - ❑ A little pressure
   - ❑ No pressure

3. Check out these statements and give your opinion with a **Y (yes)**, **N (no)**, or **M (maybe)**.
   ___ Most people my age have already been in a relationship.
   ___ You need to be in a relationship with the opposite sex to be popular.
   ___ If you aren't attractive, forget about having a boyfriend or girlfriend.
   ___ Girls and guys my age should be friends, but not boyfriend and girlfriend.
   ___ A relationship with someone of the opposite sex can help you grow as a Christian.
   ___ A young person's parents should approve of any relationship with the opposite sex.
   ___ Girls are too pushy in relationships with guys.
   ___ You should know someone a long time before getting into a close relationship with them.

4. Do you think these statements are **T (true)** or **F (false)**?
   When teenagers are in relationships—
   ___ they talk on the phone a lot.
   ___ they are more popular.
   ___ their parents become more strict.
   ___ they have more fun.
   ___ they waste a lot of time.
   ___ they end up going too far sexually.
   ___ they fight a lot with parents and friends.
   ___ they can't spend as much time with their friends.
   ___ they have to sneak around a lot.
   ___ they spend lots of time with the other person.

5. How do these verses relate to **boyfriend-girlfriend relationships** for junior high or middle school students?
   1 Kings 11:1-4
   Romans 12:9-11
   1 Corinthians 10:23-24

MORE THAN FRIENDS [boyfriends and girlfriends]

THIS WEEK

This TalkSheet will let you talk with your kids about dating and the pressures they face. You may want to consider separating the boys and the girls for the TalkSheet discussion, then bringing them together for a process time and wrap-up.

Be sensitive to the fact that some kids aren't in relationships yet or aren't allowed to be. And keep in mind that if they do date, their dating relationships aren't the same as high school dating relationships.

For more information and discussion topics, see Mission Impossible? (page 77) and Too Much Too Soon (page 73).

OPENER

How do romantic relationships differ from friendships? Ask the group to create a list of all the things boyfriends and girlfriends do while they're together (besides anything physical!). The list could include things like talking on the phone, going to the mall, hanging out with friends, going to the movies, or hanging out at school. See how big a list you can generate. Then ask your kids if these activities are the same—or different—than what they do with friends. What makes a romantic relationship different from a friendship? You may also want to rank these activities with your group on a scale of 1-5 (1 being the best activities to do with a boyfriend or girlfriend). Are some activities better than others? Why or why not?

THE DISCUSSION, BY NUMBERS

1. What ages did your kids choose? What are the pros and cons of each age? You may want to clarify the terms they use to describe relationships and various levels of a relationship (such as going together, dating, going out, hanging out, and so on).

2. How much pressure is there at your kids' schools? Why or why not? Take some time to talk about why relationships seem so important to junior highers or middle schoolers. Be sensitive to those who don't have boyfriends or girlfriends. Point out that there's nothing wrong with waiting until high school (or even college) to get romantically involved with someone.

3. You'll find it easy to create a debate with these statements. Explore with the group why boyfriend-girlfriend relationships seem so important. Then discuss the result of not being involved in a boyfriend-girlfriend relationship in junior high. What are the positives and negatives?

4. This activity shows the ups and downs in a dating relationship. Address each issue with the students. How common are these among their peers? Which ones aren't listed?

5. How do these passages relate to romantic relationships? What do your kids think God's view of dating is?

THE CLOSE

Some adults think that teenagers grow up too fast when they start to date. Statistics suggest that kids who start dating at a young age have premarital sex earlier than others. Still, junior high guys and girls are hanging out and getting involved with each other.

On the other hand, some adults see junior high dating as harmless training for future involvements. With this in mind it's important that you balance the two perspectives. Be sure to affirm those kids who don't want to have boyfriend-girlfriend relationships—and those who are already involved.

Take some time to talk about healthy dating activities and what God says about respecting and treating those of the opposite sex. What are some dangers girls and guys face when they "go out"? You may want to take some time to pray for and with your kids—and for their dating relationships.

MORE

● Show some clips of TV shows or movies in which there are dating situations. Talk about these clips and what was portrayed. What were the intentions of both people? What messages were given about dating and sex? Encourage your kids to keep their eyes open for mixed messages and pressures from the media.

● Cases of date rape and physical abuse are on the rise. You may want to discuss safe ways to date. Point out that date rape is a crime—no one, under any circumstances, can force another person into sex. What are ways your young people can protect themselves from becoming a victim? Encourage them to date in social places where there are other people. Finally, communicate that if they are ever hit, pressured into sex, or raped, they must find a trusted adult to talk to—you, a pastor, teacher, counselor or parent. For more information, visit the Rape, Abuse, and Incest National Network (www.rainn.org) or National Coalition Against Sexual Assault (http://ncasa.org).

BELIEVE IT OR NOT

1. Which of the following **doctrines** do you think are based on the Bible? (circle 'em)

Anarchy   Baptism
Hedonism   Incarnation
Justification   Pantheism
Predestination   Salvation
Atonement   Darwinism
Imputation   Islam
Materialism   Pessimism
Regeneration   Stewardship

2. Okay, time for something easier! Check the doctrines below that you know **little** or **nothing about**.

- ❑ Sin
- ❑ Redemption
- ❑ Grace
- ❑ Christ's return
- ❑ Angels

- ❑ Demons
- ❑ Heaven
- ❑ Spiritual gifts
- ❑ Creation
- ❑ Hell

- ❑ The inspiration of the Bible
- ❑ The resurrection
- ❑ The Trinity
- ❑ The church

3. What is your reaction to these statements—**Y (yes)** or **N (no)**?

___ What you believe about God and the Bible affects the way you live your life.
___ I'm not intellectual enough to understand doctrine.
___ Biblical doctrine can help people with their problems.
___ Knowing biblical doctrine makes me a Christian.
___ I didn't know the Bible had doctrines in it.
___ Biblical doctrine is only for pastors and college professors.
___ Knowing biblical doctrine will keep me from being deceived by worldly beliefs.

4. What do these verses say about doctrine?
Ephesians 4:14
1 Timothy 4:16
Titus 1:9

BELIEVE IT OR NOT [b i b l i c a l   d o c t r i n e]

THIS WEEK

Since young people have so many concerns and problems, youth workers often focus on topical studies of the Bible—like those in this book. Most spend relatively little time on doctrine, even though it is part of the foundation for spiritual maturity and stability. This TalkSheet examines the importance of biblical doctrine and helps your group identify the areas they would like to study.

OPENER

You may want to illustrate the point of this TalkSheet by bringing in a pair of sunglasses. How does wearing sunglasses affect your sight? What if you wear blue or red lenses in the glasses? Point out to the group that the Bible is like a pair of sunglasses—by reading it and knowing it, you can understand and discern false beliefs and teachings. With the Bible as a backup for their faith and what they believe, they will be able to see false religious beliefs differently.

THE DISCUSSION, BY NUMBERS

1. The areas of doctrine from the Bible are atonement, baptism, imputation, incarnation, justification, predestination, regeneration, salvation, and stewardship. You may want to use a dictionary to look up the beliefs that are not based on the Bible, and a Bible dictionary to look up those that are. Share the definitions with your students.

2. Ask the students to share their choices and why they would like to know more. Take note of their answers—you may want to plan future studies on the areas they mention. If they already know about some of these, where did they learn them?

3. How can an understanding of Christian doctrine help you live a Christian life? Point out that what you believe affects how you live. For example, those who don't believe in heaven or hell will live differently than those who do.

4. Take some time to go over these verses with your group. Some of them may have questions about them. Then see if your group can come up with one statement about doctrine based on the three passages. (For example, "Knowing doctrine can help you live the Christian life.")

THE CLOSE

You may want to go back to your introductory illustration. Tell the group that you have to put sunglasses on every time you're in the sun—to protect your eyes from the sun and to keep the glare out of your eyes. In the same way, the study of biblical doctrine is like those sunglasses—it can help you discern and protect you from false doctrines, but it must be studied again and again. Challenge your kids to put on their sunglasses—study the Bible and Christian beliefs—in order to stand up to deceptive teaching both in the world and in the church.

MORE

- You may want to have your kids do some research on the Internet for information on Christian doctrines from the list in item 2. Some of these can be pretty heavy subjects—be sure not to overload them! You may want to make this a group effort. Or you may want to have your senior pastor or someone else come in to explain these doctrines better.

- Do your kids know what a creed is? Do they have their own personal creed? Using the Apostle's Creed (or another one), have them write a creed—a statement of their personal beliefs. Encourage them to write a creed and put it in a visible place and read it when they start to doubt their beliefs or have people question what they believe and why.

HELP WANTED

1. How much **time** do you spend each week helping people outside of your family? An hour? 15 minutes? 5 minutes?

2.
> Volunteers Wanted: We're looking for people to help those in need! Jobs available in a wide variety of areas. No minimum age requirement. Eternal rewards! No experience needed. Your participation is critical. Apply today! Call 1-800-555-MINISTRY.

What do you **like most** about this want ad?

What do you **like least** about the ad?

3. Which statement summarizes your opinion about Christian service projects? **Check one.**
   - ❑ I'd participate in a Christian service project if it takes a little bit of time and work.
   - ❑ I'd participate in a Christian service project if it takes some time and work every month.
   - ❑ I'd participate in a Christian service project if it takes some time and work every week.
   - ❑ Forget it, count me out, no way—I don't want to get involved.

4. If you could be part of any **two** service projects listed below, which ones would you choose? (Feel free to list a few of your own ideas, too.)
   - ❑ Reading the Bible or books to senior citizens in a nursing home
   - ❑ Collecting clothes and blankets for homeless in your town
   - ❑ Raising money to build a playground for an inner city church day-care center
   - ❑ Taking food baskets to hungry families
   - ❑ Organizing a sports tournament to raise money for a charity
   - ❑ Traveling to Mexico to help build houses
   - ❑ Buying or collecting toys for children who can't afford them
   - ❑ Talking with AIDS patients in the hospital
   - ❑ Preparing and serving food at a rescue mission or soup kitchen
   - ❑ Organizing a party for kids in a children's home or orphanage
   - ❑ Volunteering to help with the Special Olympics
   - ❑ Tutoring children are in the hospital or orphanage
   - ❑ Other—

5. **Circle** the verses below that are examples of Christian service.

Genesis 50:21	Luke 10:30-32
Psalm 109:16	John 13:4, 5
Haggai 1:5, 6	Acts 5:1, 2
Matthew 19:21	Acts 9:36
Matthew 25:41-43	1 Corinthians 10:33

HELP WANTED [Christian service]

THIS WEEK

Has your group ever participated in Christian service? These can be life-changing experiences. Junior high and middle school kids can and should be encouraged to participate in Christian service—there's a lot they can do! This TalkSheet will give you a chance to talk about this topic with your group and possibly decide as a group to find ways of serving others on a regular basis.

OPENER

You may want to start by asking some questions specific to your area to test your group's knowledge of local community services. Use the following questions—

- Where would a woman and her children go if they were victims of domestic violence?
- Where could a 15-year-old girl go if she was pregnant and didn't know what to do?
- Where could parents of a developmentally disabled preschool child turn for help?
- Where would a family of five turn to for emergency financial assistance?
- Where is a local children's home or orphanage?
- Where could a homeless person go for food?

Divide into small groups and pass out the questions—possibly different lists of questions—along with several local telephone directories. See what resources the groups come up with. Are there different resources for each question (i.e. is there more than one homeless shelter)?

For a different intro, divide the students into small groups and distribute newspapers. Ask them to find examples of volunteer service and examples of issues and problems in need of volunteer help.

THE DISCUSSION, BY NUMBERS

1. Some of your kids may exaggerate the number of hours they spend helping others. Ask the students to give specific examples of how they help others, then ask them to identify the needs that they are ignoring each week.

2. Let the group members share the pros and cons of volunteering to serve others. How can people get over the negative aspects of serving?

3. Get a group consensus of their willingness and desire to serve. You may want to keep track of their responses for future planning of a service project.

4. Write their answers on the whiteboard or poster board. Then you may want to ask for additional suggestions of service projects to add to your list.

5. What did your kids learn from these verses? Ask them to relate what they learned from the passages addressing Christian service and the passages addressing selfishness.

THE CLOSE

Serving others is the best way to show our love for the Lord and for others. Even though there's sin and suffering, your kids can do their part to help those in need. Reaching out to those in need helps others—and also teaches people who they are. Some service experiences can be life-changing! Point out that being a Christian is more that just believing in God—it means being willing work for the good of others (Titus 2:7, 8; 3:8). Finally, you may want to close by reading Matthew 25:31-46.

MORE

- As a group, you may want to consider sponsoring a needy child through a Christian organization. There are several organizations, including World Vision (www.wvi.org) or Compassion International (www.ci.org). By doing small fundraisers or pooling their money, your kids will be able to help a child in need and experience first-hand how to support someone in need.
- Challenge your kids to get out there and do something! With your group, plan a service project oroutreach to help those in need. Take a look at the answers to item 4 for ideas. Another useful resource for planning is the *Ideas Library: Camps, Retreats, Missions & Service Ideas* (Youth Specialties).

WWW.X-RATED.SIN

1. If you saw a warning sign (something like "contains explicit sexual content") on an Internet site, what would you do?
   - ❏ See what kind of Web site it was first
   - ❏ Check to see if there was an age restriction
   - ❏ Immediately close the site
   - ❏ Think it was a joke
   - ❏ Ignore the warning—I can look at what I want
   - ❏ Tell my parent or adult who checks the history of the Internet files
   - ❏ Lie when it asks for my age, agree to the conditions, and start surfing

2. How common are the following in the lives of you or your friends—**N (never)**, **R (rarely)**, or **E (everyday)**?
   - ___ Hearing swear words or vulgar language
   - ___ Watching R-rated movies
   - ___ Listening to music with sexual lyrics
   - ___ Hearing or telling dirty jokes
   - ___ Using swear words or vulgar language
   - ___ Laughing at profanity
   - ___ Watching TV shows that are sexually explicit
   - ___ Looking at Internet or magazine pornography

3. Check out these statements and decide if you **A (agree)** or **(D) disagree**.
   - ___ You have to swear to be popular.
   - ___ You should avoid music with profane language—profanities stick in your head.
   - ___ Watching movies with vulgar language has no effect on me.
   - ___ Adults use vulgar language and swear words more than people my age.
   - ___ Christians should be upset about obscenity in the world.
   - ___ Telling dirty jokes is just harmless fun.
   - ___ It's impossible not to swear at my school.
   - ___ TV shows are becoming more obscene.
   - ___ Listening to music with sexually explicit lyrics hurts my morals.

4. How would you respond to each of the following situations?
   - Your friends listen to CDs with sexually graphic lyrics.
   - You find a *Playboy* at your best friend's house.
   - While surfing the Internet your friend keyword-searches *sex* and *nudity* to look at some very explicit Web pages.
   - A friend starts to forward dirty jokes to your e-mail address.
   - You hear your dad swearing a lot.

5. Check out these verses—what does each one say about living in an **X-rated world**?

Philippians 4:8-9	1 Timothy 4:12
1 Corinthians 6:19-20	Titus 1:15-16

WWW.X-RATED.SIN [vulgarity and pornography]

THIS WEEK

Kids today aren't sheltered. Teenagers can find vulgarity and pornography on the Internet with one click of a mouse—or by simply checking out the magazine racks at the nearest store. This TalkSheet gives you the opportunity to talk with your kids about the affect that obscenity has on their lives. For more discussion on pornography, look at Smut World (pg. 97).

OPENER

On a poster board or whiteboard write the following words—obscene, vulgar, lewd, dirty, pornographic, and filthy. Then ask the group to tell you what they think of when they see these words.

What do they think the word obscene means? Read a dictionary definition of obscene, such as Webster's New World Dictionary, which defines it as "offensive to modesty or decency; lewd."

How about the other words? You may want to ask them for examples of obscenity in your community, in their lives, at their schools, or from the media.

As you open this discussion, do be sensitive to these topics. Some of your kids may be involved with pornography. Challenge the group to handle this discussion honestly and maturely. Be sure to mediate this discussion carefully.

THE DISCUSSION, BY NUMBERS

1. If they're honest, some will admit that they've seen objectionable material on the Web. Do they pay attention to the warning signs? (If there are any.) How would they handle this situation? Do they understand how easy it is to click on the mouse and find these materials? Discuss with them how they can be discerning with what they see, hear, and read on the Web and in other media, too.

2. You may want to approach this in a general way. For example, how frequently do these happen in the lives of junior highers and middle schoolers? Have they had any direct experience with these? You may want to take anonymous votes on each of these to see what their experiences are.

3. If you open this up for debate, you'll probably get a wide variety of opinions. Do your kids think or know that obscenity has an impact on their everyday lives? Talk about why the world in which they live has become so obscene. How does today's society compare with that of their grandparents? Or their parents? What will it be like for the future generation? What can be done to put a handle on this obscenity?

4. These attention-getters make great role-play situations as well as discussion starters for handling everyday situations involving the obscene. Have your kids faced similar situations? What would be practical Christian responses to these real dilemmas?

5. How can these verses help a Christian evaluate the world? How could your kids use this verse in their own lives? What does God have to say about watching, hearing, or listening to obscene materials?

THE CLOSE

You may want to ask your group to think of an average young teenager—both a guy and a girl. What are some of the attitudes and behaviors of these average middle schoolers? What do they watch, listen to, or hear? Mention things that your kids have brought up during your discussion (things like viewing R-rated movies, reading dirty jokes, cussing, and so on). Now ask the group to predict the kind of life this person may live as they grow older—
- What kind of relationship with God will they have?
- What kind of parent will they be?
- What kind of values will they adopt?
- How will these two people treat others?
- How will they handle dating relationships?
- What will they teach their kids about vulgarity and pornography?

Encourage your kids to get grounded in God. The way to avoid temptation is to ask for God's strength—it's the Holy Spirit that provides self-control and discernment. Close with a time of prayer and challenge your kids to ask God for strength and forgiveness.

MORE

- To take this further, ask the group to give examples, from a movie, a TV show, lyrics, a standup comedy routine and so on, of what they would consider to be obscene or vulgar. What makes each of these questionable? What message do these give to middle schoolers? Do your kids notice that the more they watch this, the less sensitive to vulgarity they are?
- You may want to talk with your group about how to handle pornography. It is an addiction—in a sense, a visual drug. Teenage boys in particular struggle with these temptations. Discuss how easy it is to get hooked and what the dangers are. How does pornography affect their relationships? How they see the opposite sex? What do they think of love and intercourse? For more information, check out Caught By the Web (www.caughtbytheweb.com), Focus on the Family's resources (www.pureintimacy.org), or Breaking Free From Pornography (www.porn-free.org).

NO PLACE TO CALL HOME

1. What do you think about **homelessness**?
   I think homelessness is—
   - ❑ increasing—but not in my hometown
   - ❑ growing all over the country and world
   - ❑ staying about the same—it's always a problem
   - ❑ decreasing—there are more homeless shelters now

2. Circle your **usual response** when you see or interact with a homeless person.

Fear	Helplessness	Sympathy
Sadness	Confusion	Frustration
Thankfulness	Humility	Joy
Pride	Anger	Concern
Disgust	Repulsion	Hesitation

3. Which of these phrases do you think are **untrue** about homeless people?
   Homeless people—
   - ❑ are lazy
   - ❑ can't get a good job
   - ❑ have had a streak of bad luck
   - ❑ have children outside of marriage
   - ❑ are usually dirty and sick
   - ❑ have AIDS or HIV
   - ❑ are smarter than other people
   - ❑ are orphans or don't have families
   - ❑ aren't loved by God
   - ❑ aren't well educated

4. What's your opinion? Check the statements that you agree with.
   - ❑ There are homeless people in our community.
   - ❑ There are homeless young people my age in our community.
   - ❑ Most people don't care about the homeless.
   - ❑ Homelessness is the government's problem, not mine.
   - ❑ There's nothing that I can do to help the homeless.
   - ❑ If Christians don't help the homeless, no one will.
   - ❑ Churches should do more to help the homeless.
   - ❑ There are people in my school who are homeless

5. Check out the following verses—what does each say in your own words?
   Proverbs 14:21
   Proverbs 14:31
   Proverbs 29:7
   Proverbs 31:9

NO PLACE TO CALL HOME [homeless people]

THIS WEEK

Junior highers and middle schoolers generally are well aware of the problem of homelessness. If they live in cities they see people aimlessly walking the streets, the "will work for food" signs, and reports of the problem on the news. Homelessness is a visible problem in the United States and other parts of the world. But even though the problem is readily recognized, it's quite misunderstood. Use this TalkSheet to help clear up misconceptions about the issue and to challenge your students to become part of the solution in the name of Jesus.

OPENER

You may want to have someone unknown to the group impersonate a homeless person. This person should play and dress the part—and be able to address the issues of homelessness and answer difficult questions your kids might have. Some of these may include why they can't get a job or what made them homeless.

For a different twist, you could also ask the manager or someone from a homeless shelter to come in and talk about the problem with the group. Because they have firsthand experience, they may be able to share stories about and discuss the problems of a homeless family—food, shelter, medical care, spiritual problems, life-threatening problems, and so on.

Or you may want to ask the group to list all the things that they are thankful for. What do they have that a homeless person might not have? What small luxuries do your kids enjoy daily that they take for granted—such as a hot shower or extra snacks. Make a master list of what they are thankful for and what they have been blessed with.

THE DISCUSSION, BY NUMBERS

1. How do your kids perceive of the problem of homelessness? Take a vote and discuss why they chose their answers.

2. How many of the kids have ever talked with a homeless person? Let the group share the different feelings they have about the homeless. Why do they have these feelings? What do they think causes homelessness?

3. This will address some of the myths about homelessness. Most homeless people are not lazy—they are victims of unfortunate situations like unemployment, chronic mental illness, alcoholism, drug addiction, AIDS, single parenting, and difficult physical disabilities. Some people think that the homeless have put themselves on

the streets through their own bad choices and that they don't deserve compassion. What do your kids think about this idea? What would Christ think about it? What responsibilities do Christians have concerning this widespread social problem?

4. As the kids share their answers, you may want to debate the more controversial issues. Do they have any experiences or stories to share? Are there any other myths of homelessness that aren't listed here?

5. What do these passages say about homelessness? How can these verses be applied to the problem today?

THE CLOSE

The problem of homelessness arises from a multitude of conditions—alcoholism, drug addiction, unemployment, chronic mental illness, physical disabilities, AIDS, domestic violence, single-parent families, and government policies on welfare and affordable housing—just to name a few. Some homeless people don't want help—they prefer their chosen lifestyle—but most want help desperately. But government assistance and homeless shelters aren't enough.

Emphasize that many homeless need much more than just shelter—they need understanding and compassion. Take a look at how Christ handled the outcast (the homeless type) in the Bible, such as the lepers (see Mark 1:40-41 or Matthew 8:2-3). How can your kids as Christians show compassion to those that are homeless?

MORE

● Consider role-playing homeless situations with your kids. Give each of them a specific problem, such as losing their job, getting divorced, suddenly becoming a single parent, suffering from AIDS, being abused at home, getting hooked on cocaine, or being forced into prostitution. How would they answer those who asked, "What's wrong with you?" How would these situations affect their lives? You may want to have other kids question them and see what it's like for the homeless person to explain where they are and why.

● Or you and a few of your kids may want to dress the part and sit on a corner asking for food or money. (Be sure to get other adults to help you out and keep an eye on your kids.) How do other people react to them? What looks do they get and how to they feel? Did holding a homeless sign or "will work for food" help them? Debrief with the group and talk about experiencing homelessness from the other side.

GROWING DEEPER

1. Do you agree with this statement?
Growing as a Christian means a person
has to give up having fun.

2. Complete this statement in your own words.
Christians should want to grow as Christians because—

3. Of the list that follows, pick the **top four**. In order to grow as a Christian you should—
- ❏ tell others about Christ
- ❏ read the Bible on a regular basis
- ❏ never sin again
- ❏ learn about biblical doctrine
- ❏ be confirmed
- ❏ find a spiritual mentor
- ❏ pray
- ❏ get baptized
- ❏ become a member of a church
- ❏ help others willingly
- ❏ tithe money to the church
- ❏ have only Christian friends
- ❏ memorize Bible verses
- ❏ read some Christian books
- ❏ feel guilty most of the time
- ❏ worship God
- ❏ admit your sins
- ❏ believe in Jesus Christ
- ❏ live what you believe
- ❏ go to youth group
- ❏ other—

4. Do you think these statements are **T (true)** or **F (false)**?
___ I've spent time trying to understand Christianity.
___ I only pray in church and nowhere else.
___ I think about how Jesus would want me to deal with my problems.
___ I read my Bible in places besides church.
___ I've talked with my friends about what it means to be a Christian.
___ I'm regularly involved in activities at church.
___ I've helped someone in need during the past month.
___ I pray about what's going on in my life.
___ I think Christianity is one of the most important influences in my life.
___ I've never experienced God's love and forgiveness.
___ I realize I need God's continual grace and love.
___ I attend church more than once a week.
___ I've talked with another Christian regarding my sins.

5. Check out these verses—what do you think is the common theme of them all?

Luke 2:52	1 Peter 2:2
Ephesians 4:14, 15	2 Peter 3:18

GROWING DEEPER [Christian growth]

THIS WEEK

Young teens are capable of becoming like Jesus, and Christlikeness is what Christian growth is all about. For too long the church has neglected this age group's inner, spiritual growth, focusing instead on Bible memorization and quiz teams. Use this TalkSheet as an opportunity to evaluate how well you are meeting the spiritual growth needs of your group.

OPENER

For this introduction you will need to gather a variety of toys for different age levels, such as—

- a rattle
- a doll
- some Legos
- a Barbie doll
- a pair of roller blades
- a soccer ball or basketball
- a tennis racket
- golf clubs
- a squeaky toy
- some action figures
- a water gun
- a board game

If you don't have time or access to these—ask a friend to help who's a parent with young children.

Start out by writing the names of each item on 3x5 cards (or you can use pictures of each, too). Then place the items at random on a table and tell the group that these items are appropriate for three different age groups—babies, children (in elementary school), and adults. What do they suggest the appropriate age group is for each item? What are their reasons for their decisions? Some might include things like "it's not safe for a baby" or "adults think it's boring."

Explain to your group that just as people grow and mature into different levels of recreation and play, people also grow and mature spiritually—overcoming certain struggles and taking on new challenges with each growth spurt.

THE DISCUSSION, BY NUMBERS

1. Christian growth is not boring! How could your kids become more like Jesus while having fun? Jesus came to set them free and to give them life—Christ never intended following him to be a bore.

2. Why do some people want to grow as Christians? You might get some different answers.

3. Which of these is essential for Christian growth? You may want to ask how teenagers and adults can grow together in Christ. Why do churches have youth groups? What about summer camps or Bible studies? How do adults grow differently than kids?

4. Everyone grows at a different rate and at different times. You may want to ask your kids about their growth. How many feel like they are growing? Why or why not? What makes them grow more?

5. Take a look at each passage and together with the group, decide what the theme is. What does it say about Christian growth?

THE CLOSE

When people talk about Christian growth, they typically focus on an individual's responsibility to become more like Jesus. But people also grow in Christ through community, which is one reason for the establishment of the church. The context for growth is the living body of Christ, with Christ as the head. Take time to close the session by examining with your students how the church can better promote its spiritual growth.

MORE

● It's important for everyone to have spiritual goals. If you feel it's appropriate, ask each of your youth (or those who want to) to write a letter stating their spiritual goals and how they want to grow as Christians. Give them envelopes, which they will address to themselves and seal. Mail the letters to them anywhere from six months to a year later.

● Do your kids want to get involved and learn more? You may want to start a small group Bible study and discussion with those who are interested. Check out www.YouthSpecialties.com for some study tools, including the Creative Bible Lessons or Wild Truth series. You'll also find links to student Web sites (such as www.christianteens.net or www.teens4god.com) where your kids can download devotions, find information, and learn more about how to grow in their faith.

WAGING WAR

1. **Do you know someone who has fought in a war?**

   Which war was it?

   Have you heard stories about it?

2. **When you see or read about reports of war on TV, newspaper, or on the Internet, what do you think about? What concerns you most when you hear these reports?**

3. Circle your top **three sources** of information about war from the list below.

Teachers	Books
Internet	Church
Newspapers	Friends
TV news	Movies
Grandparents	Magazines
Parents or guardians	Other—

4. **What do you think—Y (yes) or N (no)?**
   ___ War isn't a problem in the world today.
   ___ Some video games promote war.
   ___ I would be willing to fight in a war someday.
   ___ Some reasons for wars are better than others.
   ___ Kids should be discouraged from playing with war-type toys.
   ___ Teenagers shouldn't be concerned about war.
   ___ War isn't God's will.

5. Read and rewrite James 4:1-2 in your own words.

WAGING WAR [w a r]

THIS WEEK

Teenagers play war-related video games, watch war movies, and see news coverage of wars around the world. They generally have a distorted and glorified picture of war. But war is about death and destruction, evil and pain, plunder and starvation, tragedy and tears. This TalkSheet gives your kids the chance to examine a realistic, biblical view of war. An additional TalkSheet covering the topic of nuclear war can be found on page 39.

If you or your church takes a strong position on either side of the war and peace issue, you may use this discussion as a way to help your kids understand your view as well as to form one of their own.

OPENER

For a fun and fast-paced opener, break your kids into small groups. Give each group a piece of paper and something to write with. Then give each group one minute to write down as many war movie titles as possible. For each correct war movie title, each team gets a point. The team with the most points gets a prize of your choice. Compare these titles and ask the kids what each movie is about. How does each portray war? What was the theme of the movie? Do they remember which war the movie was about? Do your kids think these movies accurately portray war?

For an extensive list of all war movie titles, check out the Internet Movie Database at http://us.imdb.com/.

THE DISCUSSION, BY NUMBERS

1. How many people do your kids know who have been in a war? What stories have they heard? What impression about war have they gotten from these people?

2. Create a master list of the group's responses. Circle those responses that are common within the group. What is it about war that gives them those reactions? Is it how the story is presented?

3. Kids usually report hearing the most about war from the media—which is okay, but usually not entirely accurate. Where do your kids learn or hear about war? What have they learned in school about war?

4. Take a poll on each answer and leave room for debate on those issues. Why do they feel the way they do?

5. What does this verse say about war? What is their impression of war from this verse?

THE CLOSE

War is sometimes inevitable to keep world peace and protect the countries of the world. War is the price people pay for freedom and justice. Christians, in particular, should fight for and promote peace, acceptance, and love.

Don't leave this discussion in a negative light. God is still on the throne and in control of what happens in today's world. Christians can find hope in Christ as they spread his love—and your kids can begin right here where they live—on the school bus or in the cafeteria. Emphasize that each group member can be a peacemaker.

MORE

● Some of your kids may not have an accurate picture of what war is. You may want to ask someone that you know—possibly a member of your church—who has been involved in war to come in and talk to your group. Encourage your kids to ask questions about what is involved in war and the tragedies that occur.

● One cause of war is the persecution of certain ethnic or religious groups and conflict among members of one country. You may want to try a role-play game called "Romans and Christians" (going way back to the days after Christ, when the Christians were intensely persecuted…and killed). Split your group up into two groups—one of Romans and the other as Christians. It works best to play this game at night in a field, large building, or wooded area. Plant a light (a torch, candle, or fire) somewhere unknown to both groups and give each of the Romans a flashlight. The goal of the Christians is to get to the light—and the Romans want to stop them. The Romans must hunt the Christians down and if they find one, they must put them in a jail. And only way for the Christians to get out of jail is to try to "convert" the Roman jail guard by quoting Bible passages, telling a story about Christ, or singing a song. The game ends when all the Christians have made it to the light (of if you've played for a long time!).

Debrief the game and talk about how each group felt. What was scary about being hunted down? What did they learn from the role-play? What if the Christians really did lose their homes or their lives? For more info and activities on the persecution of Christians, check out *Student Underground* (www.YouthSpecialties.com)

GOT FAITH?

1. **What's your opinion?** Check which one you think is correct.
   Faith is believing in something—
   ☐ that you know isn't true
   ☐ that you can't prove
   ☐ that you can't see
   ☐ that you trust in

2. Check out these statements and decide if they're **true** or **false**.
   a. It doesn't take much faith to believe there's a God._____
   b. I'm not really sure what I believe about God._____
   c. Doubting God hurts one's faith._____
   d. It would be easier to trust in Christ if there were more evidence that he is real._____

3. Why don't some Christians your age take their faith seriously?
   Choose **three** reasons from the list below.
   ☐ Christianity isn't fun.
   ☐ Christianity may not be true.
   ☐ Christianity doesn't work in everyday life.
   ☐ Christianity is too hard.
   ☐ Christianity is irrelevant to everyday life.
   ☐ Christianity doesn't make you popular.
   ☐ Christianity gets lost in busy lives.
   ☐ Christianity doesn't make much sense.
   ☐ Christianity is boring.
   ☐ Christianity is too confusing.
   ☐ Christianity is for old people who are about to die.
   ☐ Other—

4. If you took a test that showed how seriously you lived out your faith in Jesus Christ, what **grade** do you think you'd receive—an A, B, C, D, or F?

5. Check out the following verses. What does each say to you about **faith**?
   John 20:24-29   Hebrews 11:1
   Romans 3:22   Hebrews 11:6
   Romans 10:17

From *More Junior High-Middle School TalkSheets—Updated!* by David Lynn. Permission to reproduce this page granted only for use in the buyer's own youth group. www.YouthSpecialties.com

29

GOT FAITH? [f a i t h]

THIS WEEK

Some of your junior highers or middle schoolers may have different ideas of what faith is. A few may think of a church building or a worship service. Others think of reading the Bible or believing in religion. Use this TalkSheet to explore the faith of your group of young people.

OPENER

Start this session off by having your group make two separate lists on a whiteboard or poster board—one list of things that they can be sure of, another of things that they can't be sure of. For example, your kids can be sure that the sky is blue, that milk comes from cows, and that fire is hot. But they can't be sure of things like when the world will end, what high school will be like, or when they'll die. Encourage them to brainstorm hard and write everything down—even thoughts that might be random or silly.

Now go through both lists and put check marks next to those that humans have control over (for example, "I know that I will fail if I don't study"). Then star those that others have control of ("I don't know if my teacher likes me"). Finally, circle those that God is in charge of (basically everything).

Ask your group which ones are scary to them—usually the ones they aren't sure of. What are they scared of? How do they feel, knowing they have no control over situations? What is hard about believing in something you can't see? You'll probably get answers like "because I doubt it" or "because you can't prove it." How do they feel knowing that someone has control of circumstances? Finally, what do they think faith is? Is it only believing in God or can you have faith in other things, like people or events?

THE DISCUSSION, BY NUMBERS

1. How did your kids answer these statements? What is your group putting its faith in—the church, a set of beliefs found in a book, a quest for the meaning of life, or an historical Jesus who is who he says he is?

2. Give them the opportunity to ask questions and express their doubts. Asking questions is one of the best ways to grow in the faith. Be sure to provide a safe environment and remind the group that there is no such thing as a stupid question.

3. Let the group members share their opinions. See if the group can reach a consensus on the top three reasons. How can these three be overcome?

4. How strong are your kids in their personal faith in Jesus Christ? Don't force your kids to share their grades. Instead ask them how they grade themselves in how they live their faith as a youth group. What can they do to bump that grade up?

5. What do these verses say about faith? Take time to look at the passages as a group—then form a group definition of what faith is.

THE CLOSE

Explain that many people talk about faith in terms of belief. They believe that there is a God or they believe that you should go to church. But is simple believe that faith the kind of faith God wants? There isn't anything wrong with a belief that focuses on information. The Bible says that even the demons believe (James 2:19). But there is another kind of faith—a faith that believes in something. It is based on facts, but runs deeper than mere knowledge. It focuses on a relationship with God. Your kids should understand that God didn't expect them to walk around lost and in the dark—the Bible provides them with the facts for their faith. But they still must believe in those facts to have a personal relationship with Jesus Christ.

MORE

● You may want to hold a faith Q&A time with your group. Have the kids write anonymously on 3x5 cards any questions they have about the Christian faith. Then collect the cards and have kids take turns picking out questions. If they feel comfortable, have them try to answer it or pass it on. Discuss the questions as a group and encourage them to use the Bible to answer their questions. To liven things up, invite your senior pastor to a meeting and put him in the hot seat for a question and-answer-session!

● Challenge your kids to e-mail or talk with one adult this week about belief in God, life after death, the Bible, miracles, prayer, and so on. Or, challenge them to go into an on-line chat room to get some responses on these questions. This is a great way to challenge others to think about and defend their beliefs. Especially if they enter chatrooms under non-Christian Web pages! Later have them share their experiences, what was discussed and what the kids learned from doing this.

COLORBLIND CHRISTIANITY

1. How would you complete this?
When I think of being friends with someone of another race—
   - ❏ I feel uncomfortable.
   - ❏ I don't really think about it.
   - ❏ I know that my parents wouldn't like it.
   - ❏ I'm afraid of what others would think.
   - ❏ It doesn't bother me at all.
   - ❏ I think it's cool.

2. How would you answer these—**Y (yes)** or **N (no)**?
Have you ever—
   ___ heard a joke that was racist?
   ___ felt you might be prejudiced?
   ___ heard about a racially motivated fight at your school?
   ___ participated in racial name-calling?
   ___ been prejudiced against by others?
   ___ visited a racially hateful Web site?
   ___ talked with a member of another race about Jesus Christ?

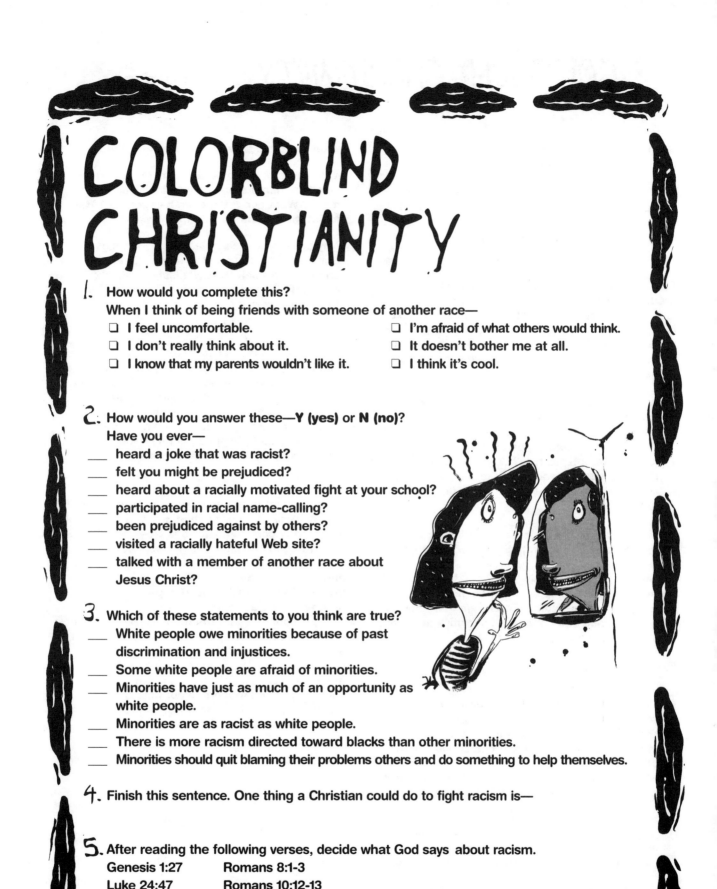

3. Which of these statements to you think are true?
   ___ White people owe minorities because of past discrimination and injustices.
   ___ Some white people are afraid of minorities.
   ___ Minorities have just as much of an opportunity as white people.
   ___ Minorities are as racist as white people.
   ___ There is more racism directed toward blacks than other minorities.
   ___ Minorities should quit blaming their problems others and do something to help themselves.

4. Finish this sentence. One thing a Christian could do to fight racism is—

5. After reading the following verses, decide what God says about racism.
Genesis 1:27	Romans 8:1-3
Luke 24:47	Romans 10:12-13
Acts 10:28	James 2:8-9

From *More Junior High-Middle School TalkSheets—Updated!* by David Lynn. Permission to reproduce this page granted only for use in the buyer's own youth group. www.YouthSpecialties.com

31

COLORBLIND CHRISTIANITY [r a c i s m]

THIS WEEK

By middle school, kids are well aware of race relations. Some will have observed situations of prejudice and bigotry, even though most will say they aren't prejudiced. Racism is a persistent problem—in the U.S. and around the world. It causes conflicts, hatred, and war. This TalkSheet will help your group examine racism in light of Christianity.

OPENER

Break the students into small groups. Ask each group to think of or create a stereotype for a specific group of people—a peer group from school (like skaters, jocks, or surfers), a race or ethnic group, or an age group like senior citizens. After each group shares the stereotypes, you may want to ask them these questions—

- What are the assumed ideas about each group?
- How common are these stereotypes among middle schoolers and people in general?
- Why do these stereotypes exist?
- Are the stereotypes true? Why or why not?
- Do these ideas help or hurt those being stereotyped?
- Do the stereotypes help you better understand a group of people?

Your kids may have a variety of answers for the opener. Some of them probably haven't taken a close look at stereotypes before.

As you go through this TalkSheet, be sensitive to members in your group who may be victims of stereotypes and prejudice. Encourage the group to be open-minded and honest, yet sensitive about how they voice their opinions and ideas.

THE DISCUSSION, BY NUMBERS

1. Depending on your community or group, some of your kids may have more contact with minorities than others. For some, this isn't an issue. The more personal and positive contact one has with other races, the less racism exists. Ask your group why some kids may—or may not—feel uncomfortable in close relationships with other races.

2. As some share their experience, ask the group why they feel some people are racist. Brainstorm what they as teens can do when they hear a racist joke or are put in similar circumstances.

3. Ask for opinions on each of these statements. These are emotional issues, so don't allow kids to put others down with their responses. Can they back up their responses with support from the Bible? Many of them have most likely not considered what the Bible says about race relations.

4. What can they do to fight racism? What are some small and large steps they as individuals can make? What about the church in general? How about their peers outside of church?

5. Why does racism exist—especially among Christians—if God created all people in his image and made his salvation available to all who accept it? What summary can the group make from these verses?

THE CLOSE

The Bible makes it clear that God is opposed to racism in any form. God clearly says that everyone is equal in his eyes. Because everyone was created equal, they should be treated equally (Numbers 15:15). Encourage your kids to see racism God's way—to oppose racism and discrimination and live in such a way that people of all races will be drawn to God's redemptive, colorblind love.

MORE

- You may want to ask your group to keep a list of observations about race relations at their schools and in their community for one week. What positive or negative things to they see, hear, or read? How often did it occur? When? What happened and how was it handled? What groups were involved? Was it just racial groups, or was a peer group involved as well?

- Or have your kids surf the Internet for information on hate groups, including skinheads, neo-Nazis, and white supremacists. You may be surprised at what your kids already know about them—they are in nearly every school across the country. Take some time to learn more about hate groups. Discuss their motives, what issues they are angry about, and what your kids can do about them.

WHO IS GOD ANYWAY?

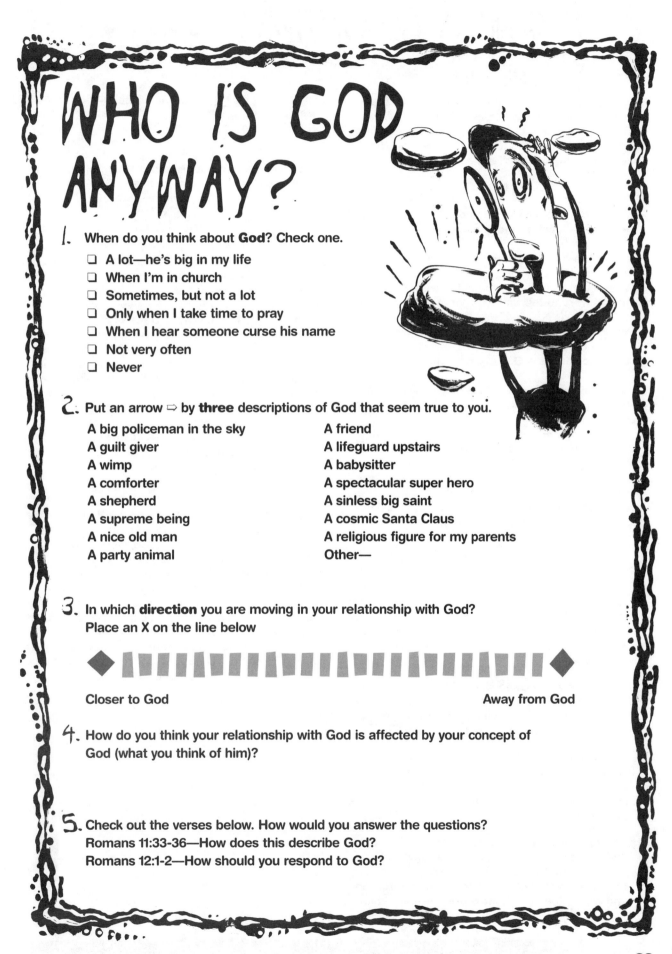

1. When do you think about **God**? Check one.
   - ❑ A lot—he's big in my life
   - ❑ When I'm in church
   - ❑ Sometimes, but not a lot
   - ❑ Only when I take time to pray
   - ❑ When I hear someone curse his name
   - ❑ Not very often
   - ❑ Never

2. Put an arrow ⇨ by **three** descriptions of God that seem true to you.

A big policeman in the sky	A friend
A guilt giver	A lifeguard upstairs
A wimp	A babysitter
A comforter	A spectacular super hero
A shepherd	A sinless big saint
A supreme being	A cosmic Santa Claus
A nice old man	A religious figure for my parents
A party animal	Other—

3. In which **direction** you are moving in your relationship with God?
   Place an X on the line below

   Closer to God   Away from God

4. How do you think your relationship with God is affected by your concept of God (what you think of him)?

5. Check out the verses below. How would you answer the questions?
   Romans 11:33-36—How does this describe God?
   Romans 12:1-2—How should you respond to God?

WHO IS GOD ANYWAY? [G o d]

THIS WEEK

No one has ever seen God—but the Bible is filled with metaphorical descriptions of him. This discussion will allow you to talk about what your students believe—what they think God is like and how their belief in God makes a difference in their lives.

OPENER

For this intro, you'll need some balloons and slips of paper, one for each of these questions—

- If God were to visit your church, where would he sit?
- What color of hair do you think God has?
- If God were to talk with you, what tone of voice would he use?
- What might God say is the funniest-looking animal he created?
- What do you think God does for fun?

Write one question on each slip of paper and put one question in each balloon. Then blow up and tie the balloon.

At the beginning of your meeting, ask for some volunteers to participate and give them each a balloon. Each person must sit on the balloon to pop it and to retrieve the question inside. Then they have to answer the statements on the slip of paper. Feel free to add more questions to vary the discussion, depending on the size and maturity of your group.

THE DISCUSSION, BY NUMBERS

1. You may want to get a show of hands or an anonymous vote for this one. Then get an overall average of how often your kids think of God. How has their view of God changed since they were younger? When and why do they think more about God?

2. Encourage your kids to share their ideas of God and to add any additional ideas as well. What misunderstandings or myths about God have they heard? → lightning shoot from eyes
Why do some people think of God differently?

3. How would your kids rate themselves on this scale? If they don't want to share, address this from a general point of view or ask for anonymous answers. Where would they put an average person their age?

4. What people think about God has an impact on their relationship with him. If you view God as mean, it'll be hard to have a close personal friendship with him. If you see God as forgiving and warm, then you'll probably open up to him more. Ask your kids how they feel about their relationship with God. How is it affected by their thoughts about him?

5. Take some time to talk about the connection between who God is (Romans 11:33-36) and what your kids' responses should be to God if they fully understand him (Romans 12:1-2).

THE CLOSE

Challenge the group to rethink their view of God. Some people have distorted views of him, which limits what God can do in their lives. He commands people not to worship idols, but to focus on him and his power. Pay attention to the views your kids have. Why have they formed these views of him? What have their parents or teachers taught them about God? Do some of them lack trust in God because of poor relationships with parents or guardians? Point out that every person has a unique relationship with God—because everyone relates to him differently!

Close in a time of prayer and encourage your kids to take a few moments with God alone. The best way to understand and get to know God better is to spend some time with him. What are some ways that your kids can get closer to God?

MORE

- Take this discussion further into the Bible. Ask the kids to pick and read five Bible stories. Read the stories with the group and have them write down five new things they learned about God.
- Consider pursuing a Bible study with some of your kids to look at the attributes of God. A recommended study for junior highers and middle schoolers is *Wild Truth Bible Lessons—Pictures of God* and *Wild Truth Journal—Pictures of God* (Youth Specialties). For more suggested resources and information, check out the Youth Specialties Web page at www.YouthSpecialties.com.

HOOKED ON DRUGS

1. **What do you think? Check one of the following.**
   - ❏ Most kids at my school don't do alcohol and other drugs.
   - ❏ Some kids are into drugs and alcohol.
   - ❏ Only a certain crowd of kids do them.
   - ❏ The majority of kids are into drugs and alcohol.

2. A gateway drug is a drug that gets people hooked on doing drugs. Check out the following list of drugs—circle the three that you think are the most frequently used "starter" drugs among peers your age (this includes "sniffing" them—like markers or paint fumes).

Alcohol	Downers	Caffeine	Inhalants
Model glue	Heroin	Marijuana	Cocaine
Tobacco	Markers	Speed	Gasoline
LSD	Paint thinner	Spray paint	

3. Why do you think the gateway drugs you identified in question 2 are used by people your age?

4. Choose the five best reasons for you to avoid alcohol and drugs and rank them from **1 (first)** to **5 (last).**
   - ___ I don't want to disappoint my parents.
   - ___ I don't want to hurt my body.
   - ___ I want to stay close to God.
   - ___ I don't want to get into trouble.
   - ___ I don't want to get addicted.
   - ___ I don't want to go against what I believe.
   - ___ I don't want to lose my friends.
   - ___ I don't want to have problems in the future.
   - ___ I don't want to get arrested.
   - ___ I want to live up to my full potential.

5. How would you avoid alcohol and other drug use?
   - ❏ Hang out with friends who don't use
   - ❏ Avoid places where people drink or use drugs
   - ❏ Stick to your decision to say no
   - ❏ Eat lots of red meat and vegetables
   - ❏ Tell people that you don't drink
   - ❏ Spend time with God in prayer
   - ❏ If you do use, only use a little bit
   - ❏ Don't go to parties
   - ❏ Chat with your parents about suggestions
   - ❏ Tell people you're a Christian.
   - ❏ Take healthy risks to have fun in life.

6. Which of the following passages is the most helpful in dealing with the issue of alcohol and drugs? Circle the one you chose and write a short sentence about why you chose it.

Proverbs 3:7, 8	1 Corinthians 3:16, 17	Galatians 6:7, 8
Proverbs 23:19-21	2 Corinthians 13:5, 6	
Luke 8:11-15	2 Romans 14:21	

HOOKED ON DRUGS [substance abuse]

THIS WEEK

Youth today are doing drugs and drinking alcohol at younger ages. Unfortunately, junior high and middle school kids don't understand that alcohol and drugs are in the same category—they're both destructive and harmful substances. And they're extremely addictive. This TalkSheet will provide an open discussion on using drugs and alcohol—and how Christian young people can resist the pressure to be users.

Be sensitive to those in your group who may have been using drugs already. Due to statistics, there most likely are a few in your group who have experimented with this stuff. Be careful not to come off sounding judgmental—keep an open mind during the discussion.

OPENER

You may want to start with a large poster board or whiteboard. On the top, write two headings—*alcohol* and *other drugs*. Ask the group to think of as many names or examples of each and keep track of the names in each column. For example, under alcohol, your kids might say things like vodka or Budweiser. For other drugs, you might get examples like cocaine, marijuana, and sniffing paint fumes. Challenge your kids to think of as many as they can—what have they heard about other kids using? How about adults? What have they seen on TV or in the movies? Keep track of the two lists for discussion.

Now go through each column and decide which one is the most common in each column among peers their age. Is there one specific drug that is easy to get? How about an alcoholic drink? Why are these two so easy for teenagers to get and use? What makes it appealing? What are the potential dangers of these two?

You may also want to ask your group to name all the sports figures, celebrities, or other famous people they know who have had problems with alcohol or drugs. What happened to these people? Where are these people today?

THE DISCUSSION, BY NUMBERS

1. Some of your kids will say that drugs and alcohol are problems for some peers. How do these kids get hooked?

2. Drugs like caffeine, tobacco, and alcohol introduce kids to chemicals. Are your kids familiar with these gateway drugs? Do they know any others that aren't on the list?

3. Why do junior highers and middle schoolers use gateway drugs? What gets them hooked? You may want to make a master list of the drugs and reasons why kids get started.

4. As you focus on good reasons to avoid use, try to reach a consensus for the best reasons to stay clean. What are the benefits and long-term rewards?

5. You may want to take time to role-play tough situations that your kids face. What happens if they're faced with one of these choices? What are the best ways to say no? Why or why not?

6. What was the most helpful passage? Are there any other stories or verses that they know of? What does God say about being drug users?

THE CLOSE

The temptations to use drugs are everywhere. As you close, affirm that it takes will power and determination to stay clean. Encourage your kids to find others to support them and encourage them—to keep them accountable for saying no. And point out that God gives power to those who ask for help in resisting temptation—check out 1 Corinthians 10:13 or James 1:12-15. Challenge your kids to make a commitment to stay clean and to find someone else who can encourage them.

MORE

● How can your kids deal with addiction? What if they have a friend who is hooked? What can they do to help themselves and others? You may want to talk more about how to handle drug abuse and the importance of breaking the addiction. For information and discussion ideas, check out the National Council on Alcoholism and Drug Dependence, Inc. (http://ncadd.org) or the Addiction Research Foundation (www.arf.org/isd/info.html).

● Or you may want to ask someone to talk about drug addiction—possibly someone who works with users, treats those who are addicted, or has recovered from drug abuse. Some of your kids may have stories of people that they know who have been hooked. Take some time to talk about these stories and what happened—but be sure to mediate the conversation. What did your kids learn from these stories? How real are the dangers of drugs and alcohol?

WALKING WITH GOD

1. On a scale of 1-10 (1 being totally true, 10 being completely untrue), how true is this statement for you?
My relationship with God is the most important relationship I have.

2. How would you feel in the following situations?
You've just been told you can never have a close relationship with God.

You've just been told you can never again attend church.

You've just been told you are wasting your time on this Christian stuff.

3. When do you feel closest to God?

I feel close to God—
- ❑ during the church worship service
- ❑ when I think about heaven
- ❑ at camps and retreats
- ❑ during Communion, the Lord's Supper
- ❑ when I pray by myself
- ❑ while reading the Bible
- ❑ when I'm at school
- ❑ during Sunday school
- ❑ on holidays, like Christmas or Easter
- ❑ when I'm in trouble
- ❑ anytime I'm at church
- ❑ at no particular time
- ❑ I don't feel close to God

4. Check the **top six things** you think would help you have a better friendship with God.
- ❑ Regularly attend church
- ❑ Take communion
- ❑ Watch TV evangelists
- ❑ Accept God's acceptance of you just the way you are
- ❑ Talk with God every day
- ❑ Keep all of God's rules
- ❑ Try really hard to please God
- ❑ Spend time with other Christians
- ❑ Spend time alone with God
- ❑ Spend time on Christian Web sites
- ❑ Reach out to help others in the name of Christ
- ❑ Thank God regularly for all the things he does for you
- ❑ Worry that God will punish you for your sins
- ❑ Read a Christian book or magazine
- ❑ Learn more about God by reading the Bible
- ❑ Feel guilty a lot
- ❑ Listen to God

5. Read each of the following verses that describe something about Jesus Christ's humanness. What did you learn about Christ being human?

Matthew 26:37	Luke 8:23
Luke 2:40	Luke 24:39
Luke 4:2	John 4:6

WALKING WITH GOD [k n o w i n g   G o d]

THIS WEEK

Everyone needs to have personal relationships. They're vital for growth and happiness, especially during the young teen years. During this time, junior highers or middle schoolers may start to think about God differently—to think of God in more personal terms, as a friend. This TalkSheet will give you the chance to talk with your group about knowing God more personally.

OPENER

For this activity you'll need markers and a white-board or a large sheet of paper (the paper should be taped to a wall where the group can see it). With suggestions from the group, ask one young person to draw a picture of God. Try to incorporate all of the suggestions into your drawing. Your kids may mention characteristics like white hair, beard, wrinkles, wise eyes, and tall body. How do they perceive God would look if he was a person? Why do they have certain ideas of what he would look like? Where have they formed these ideas? Is it hard to think of characteristics of God? Why or why not?

Now ask the group how they feel knowing that they can have a personal friendship with God himself! Is that scary? Exciting? You may want to ask the group how they understand God. How do they get to know him better and get closer to him? Feel free to ask additional questions or tweak this introduction based on the size and maturity of your group. If you have a large group, you may want to break it down into smaller groups and compare how each group drew God.

THE DISCUSSION, BY NUMBERS

1. You won't find the phrase "personal relationship with Jesus Christ" in the Bible. Yet people talk about a personal relationship with Christ in metaphors of a friend, a family member, and a spouse. Ask the kids what they think it means to have a personal relationship with God.

2. This activity lets kids examine how significant their relationship with God really is. How would they answer each of these questions?

3. Ask the group why the times they chose are special times with God, then let kids add additional times they feel close to God that aren't on the list.

4. Explore ways the group can help one another to develop a more personal relationship with God. Ask each kid to create a plan for knowing God more personally, based on what is learned as people share their lists.

5. God became human because he wanted to have a relationship with his children. Too often people dwell on God's divinity and ignore his humanity. By focusing for a minute on God's humanness, young people can appreciate the personal side of God. Read and discuss Hebrews 4:15, 16.

THE CLOSE

The metaphor of walking with God is a useful way to look at how people relate to him. There are different ways people walk when they're with others. For example, if you go to the mall with your parents, you might walk away from them. You don't want your friends to see you so close to them. When walking with a boyfriend or a girlfriend, you might hold hands or walk arm in arm. If you have the unfortunate experience of walking with a police officer to be questioned for a crime, you might walk with your head lowered. With your friends, you might walk casually as you talk. Ask the kids to describe how they are walking with God. Does their walk change from day to day? Why or why not?

There's a bumper sticker that reads "If you don't feel close to God, guess who moved." Point out to your kids that God never moves from them—they move away from God. Encourage your kids to get closer with God by drawing near to him. James 4:8 says "Come near to God and he will come near to you." Read this verse and spend some time in prayer, giving your kids time to think about God and draw near to him.

MORE

- Encourage those in your group who are interested to keep spiritual journals of their walk with God for one week. Point out that journaling is useful for writing down thoughts, prayer requests, and ideas of God. Suggest a time to journal—while reading the Bible, listening to music, during prayer, or while thinking about your day. You may want to talk about their experiences—what did they learn by journaling? Did it help their walk with God or not? If so, how?
- Illustrate a walk with God by reading the poem "Footprints in the Sand" (you can find the poem via the Internet or in *Hot Illustrations for Youth Talks* by Wayne Rice/Youth Specialties, pg. 98). You may want to read this to your group and then ask them to think about their lives. Have they felt time when God has carried them? Where are they walking now? Is God carrying them? How do they think their relationship with God will change as they get older and get closer to him? You may want to have your kids draw a picture of their footprints in the sand—when God has carried them and when they've walked alongside of God.

NUKE 'EM

1. How likely do you think is it that a **nuclear war** could destroy civilization?
   - ❑ Totally will happen
   - ❑ Definitely could happen
   - ❑ Probably could happen
   - ❑ It could never happen

2. What do you think—**yes** or **no**?
   Have you ever worried about a nuclear war happening in your lifetime?

   Have you ever thought about what it would be like if you survived a nuclear war?

   Have you ever wondered what God thinks about nuclear weapons?

3. Who have you talked about the possibility of a nuclear war with?
   - ❑ Teachers at school
   - ❑ Your parent(s)
   - ❑ Friends
   - ❑ Others your age
   - ❑ Your pastor
   - ❑ Other—

4. Do you think that the world is a safer place to live because of nuclear weapons? Why or why not?

5. Do you **A (agree)** or **D (disagree)** with the statements below?
   ___ People need to learn more about the threat of nuclear war.
   ___ The Bible has nothing to say about nuclear war.
   ___ The threat of nuclear war is one of the biggest problems faced by today's world.
   ___ There's nothing that can be done to prevent nuclear war.
   ___ Nuclear weapons could be used on a limited scale without getting out of hand.
   ___ Nuclear war isn't as big of an issue as it was a few years ago.

6. Check out the following verses—what does each have to say about nuclear war?
   Psalm 34:14
   Proverbs 12:20
   Matthew 5:9
   Romans 12:18

NUKE 'EM [nuclear war]

THIS WEEK

It's a scary thought—mankind possesses the ability to destroy this planet. Although the Cold War has ended, the threat of nuclear war comes and goes—and it still causes anxiety and fears, depending on what world crisis is occurring. This TalkSheet provides a forum for positive discussion on nuclear war and the role of Christians as peacemakers.

OPENER

To start this discussion, break the group into four smaller groups and have them sit at tables placed strategically around the room. Each group represents a country. Give each group an envelope that contains information about its country. Keep the information brief, but mention the number of nuclear weapons it has, the wealth it possesses, and the level of democracy that exists.

Place a larger table in the middle of the room to represent the United Nations. Any country can send a representative to any other country by going to another's table. When any one country wants to talk to all the countries, it can call a meeting of the United Nations and a delegate from each of the countries must gather at the middle table. Be sure to designate one country as a primarily Christian nation. Tape a list of each country's information on the United Nations table for all the countries to see. Give each country one minute to talk briefly about its information and to select a president, an ambassador to each other country, and a United Nations representative.

Announce that one of the countries has been attacked by another with nuclear weapons. Give the attacking country a sheet of paper and ask the group to write down the extent of damage done to the country they attacked. (As moderator, you are allowed to mediate this process and deny any damages, which you will want to keep to a minimum at first so that the game can continue). Tape the damage list with the name of the attacking country to the attacked country's table. Then let the game begin by allowing the attacked country as well as the other countries decide what they will do about the situation. Facilitate this process until you are satisfied that the young people have learned something about nuclear war and foreign relations.

You can discuss the activity by asking what difference Christian principles made, what difference nuclear weapons made, and what happened during the course of the game.

THE DISCUSSION, BY NUMBERS

1. Let the young people share their opinions. You can refer to what happened during the simulation game used to introduce this topic.

2. Kids will have stories that they've heard about or seen in the movies. Focus on what the young people believe God thinks about nuclear weapons.

3. The nuclear threat is one of the least talked about topics between parents and their kids. Many of the young people won't know what their parents believe. Many might talk about it in school. Why don't they talk to their parents about it? How about other adults?

4. Do they think the world is a safe place? What do they think would make the world a safer place to live?

5. Take a poll on each of these statements. Let the young people debate the more controversial issues.

6. What do these verses say about war and world peace? What do they think God has to say about nuclear war?

THE CLOSE

Fears and concerns about the growth in nuclear weapons and the threat of war are normal. But God is in control of the nations. If you look at the Old Testament, you'll clearly see that God was in control of history—even though it didn't always appear that way to his people. God wants your kids to work for peace, which can start in their hometown—at home, at school, in your neighborhood, on your sports team, and at church. Encourage your kids to pray for the powerful countries of the world and for wisdom of world leaders.

MORE

- You may want to ask your kids to make a list of all the movies they've seen where nuclear war was a threat. Does your group think that these movies accurately describe the threat of war? Why or why not? What influence do they think media has on how people think of war and nuclear weapons?
- Check out some on-line information about nuclear war and weapons. There are several Web pages with simulation maps and more. Challenge your kids to find some new information about nuclear war by doing a keyword search of or check out http://www.pbs.org/wgbh/amex/bomb/.

PLUGGED IN

1. How many years have you been going to church?

2. On a scale of 1-10 (1 being not involved at all, 10 being very involved), how involved are you in your church (doing things like volunteering in the nursery, helping with the youth group)?

   What are you involved in and why?

   How involved in church will you be when you're in **high school**?
   - ❑ More involved than I am now
   - ❑ About the same as I am now
   - ❑ Less involved than I am now

3. Check the statements that you think are **true**.
   Teenagers who are involved in church—
   - ❑ have an easier time with their lives
   - ❑ act like their lives are perfect
   - ❑ have more friends
   - ❑ don't do drugs or drink alcohol
   - ❑ only listen to music by Christian artists
   - ❑ get brownie points with the youth pastor
   - ❑ have fun while doing it and feel rewarded
   - ❑ will get closer to God than others

4. If I could change **anything** at my church, I would—

5. What do you think—**yes** or **no**?
   ___ I regularly attend church.
   ___ My parents and I generally agree about church attendance.
   ___ I like being involved in church.
   ___ I'm committed to our church.
   ___ Church is important for kids my age and adults.
   ___ I think it's more important to be at church than youth group.
   ___ I help out in some way at church on a regular basis.
   ___ I don't think young people should have to do work at church.
   ___ I wish I didn't have to attend church at all.

6. Look up **Acts 2:42-47** in a Bible. What do you think it would've been like to attend the kind of church described?

PLUGGED IN [church involvement]

THIS WEEK

Going to church hasn't been a option for many junior highers and middle schoolers. Some have gone to church since birth, but they're fast approaching an age where they can make a choice about their involvement. Some of your kids love church involvement—others do everything they can to get out of it. This TalkSheet will give you an opportunity to talk about church involvement in a non-threatening way.

Try to let kids who are rebelling against attending church to speak their mind—they may have some ideas that may help you to understand your kids and your church better. Encourage those who are excited and actively involved to share why they like being involved. Keep an open environment for listening to feedback, opinions, and ideas.

OPENER

This introductory activity will encourage some creative thought from your kids about how they see the church. Divide your kids into groups of four or five. Give each group an item like a coat hanger, a chair, an eraser, or a roll of masking tape. Then ask each group to think up a one-statement slogan related to the item that describes the church. For example, if the item were a coat hanger, the group might say something like "Church is like a coat hanger; if you use it, you'll have less wrinkles in your life." If you choose not to hand out specific items, you can ask the group to come up with a slogan using any item. For example, a group may say "Church is like a cellular phone; whenever you need it, it's there."

THE DISCUSSION, BY NUMBERS

1. You may want to total up these answers for a grand total of years your kids have attended church. Take a look at this and estimate how many sermons your kids have sat through. How many do they remember?

2. How did your kids rate their involvement? For those who ranked themselves high, what are they involved in? Do they enjoy it? Why or why not? Ask you kids for some reasons for their responses and identify the trend in your group. Are most expecting to exit or get more involved?

3. Here are some statements about practical Christianity and the teenager. Which of these statements did your kids agree with? Why or why not? What are some assumptions of teenagers in the church?

4. Without letting this turn into a gripe session, provide an opportunity for your kids to give their

input on the church. What suggestions do they have? New ideas? Inspirations for church leaders? Pay close attention to their opinions—they are part of the church, too!

5. You may want to take a poll on each of these statements. Note what your group thinks about church and what makes it worthwhile.

6. Ask the students to share their answers about attending the first-century church. Then ask the group what Christians from the first-century church might say if they had the chance to attend today's church.

THE CLOSE

You may want to close this session with a brainstorming activity. Ask your kids to create a list of all the benefits of being involved in church as a teenager. Focus on worship, service opportunities, fun times, and personal Christian growth activities. This simple activity can help your young people identify all of the positive opportunities available that they have never considered.

Finally, take some time to pray for your church, the church leaders, and the youth of your church. Encourage your kids to pray for how they can get involved in the church as well.

MORE

● You may want to invite some of your church leaders to be in on this TalkSheet discussion. This is a convenient opportunity for them to hear what the youth of the church are thinking and feeling. Possibly have a question and answer session after the discussion for the pastor, elders, or committee members to bounce ideas off of your youth and vice versa. Encourage a teamwork approach to the discussion and challenge your kids to continue making suggestions and ideas to the church leaders.

● Consider holding a special service for your kids—or have your kids plan a service for the church. What would they like to see happen in this service? Would they like a sermon on a specific topic? How singing some of their favorite songs? Encourage them to get involved in the planning. Then debrief on how it was for them to be involved and whether or not they enjoyed the service.

YOUR LAST BREATH

1. How often have you thought about **death**?
   - ❑ A lot—almost daily
   - ❑ Whenever I see someone die on TV
   - ❑ A few times
   - ❑ Only at a funeral or when someone famous dies
   - ❑ Never

2. Why do you think parents teach their children prayers, like this one, about death?

   Now I lay me down to sleep,
   I pray the Lord my soul to keep.
   If I should die before I wake,
   I pray the Lord my soul to take.

3. Ethan was always very involved in his church and youth group, until last night when he died of leukemia. His seventh grade homeroom class found out about his death just minutes ago, and although they knew he had the disease, they are stunned.

   What would you say to the class to help them cope with Ethan's death?

   How would you feel if you were Ethan's parents?

   Would his death be different if he were in a car accident? Why or why not?

   How would his death affect you or those who were his friends?

4. Take a look at these statements and mark each one **T (true)** or **F (false)**.
   ___ Death is a natural part of the life cycle.
   ___ God lets some people die for no reason.
   ___ Young people shouldn't die before older people.
   ___ Death sometimes freaks me out.
   ___ The media makes too big a deal about dying.
   ___ Dying naturally is the same as committing suicide.

5. If you could ask God **one question** about dying, what would it be?

6. Check out **1 Corinthians 15:54-58**—what do you think it teaches Christians about death?

YOUR LAST BREATH [d e a t h]

THIS WEEK

Death is a topic that more and more must be talked about with kids. An increasing number of young people are preoccupied with death—in their music, through the suicide of a classmate, in their contemplation of the meaning and purpose of life, and especially in the shocking wake of school violence and killings. This TalkSheet faces death head on.

OPENER

This is a sensitive topic—especially for those who have lost someone they've loved. To start this discussion, ask who your kids have lost that they've loved.

Maybe some of your kids have lost parents, a sibling, or a grandparent. Take a few moments to talk about their deaths. You kids may have questions about why God lets people die. Death can seem unfair to kids (and adults, too).

Or have your kids think about this—if they were to die, what would people say about them? What would they hear their friends saying at their funeral? What does this say about how they live today? Why is it so important to make the most of each day?

THE DISCUSSION, BY NUMBERS

1. Many kids will share the experiences they have had with death, such as the death of a grandparent or a pet. Or perhaps they will talk about the suicide of a classmate or the death and destruction themes of some secular music. Be sensitive to young people who are mourning the loss of a friend or family member. Allow kids to share their stories and express their emotions.

2. Take this opportunity to talk about the apparent meaninglessness of death. Explain to the group that the Bible has a lot to say about death. Death was brought into the world because of sin (Romans 5:12; 6:23). The prayer was written at a time when death was more real to young people because the medical treatments available today had not yet been invented and many people died in childhood.

3. Ask your kids to share the responses they would give the students to help them cope with Ethan's death.

4. The New Testament (Romans 5:12-14; 1 Corinthians 15:26) teaches that death is our enemy, although Christians need not fear it. Death proves the reality of sin and evil. It was not originally part of God's creation.

5. Answer as many questions as you have time for. Remind the group that there is no such thing as a stupid question. Expect a wide variety of questions from cremation to reincarnation and more.

6. Study the passage together, focusing on the Christian's hope in death (our Savior, Jesus Christ) and the response to this hope, which should be to stand firm and serve the Lord forever.

THE CLOSE

Point out to your group that the life of each person has meaning. It's God who gives their lives meaning—and because of Christ's death on the cross, each of your kids can be saved from the despair of a death. Through the salvation offered by Jesus, Christians can pass from death into life—a life everlasting (John 5:24). As you close, reassure your kids of the love that God has for them. Take some time to wrap up the discussion and close with a time of prayer with your group for comfort and hope for the future.

MORE

- Suicide is a reality in the lives of teenagers—one of the top five causes of death among teenagers and young adults. You may want to spend some time talking about suicide, what causes teen suicide, how to recognize someone who is in danger of taking his or her own life. Visit a few on-line organizations for more information—Suicide Voices Awareness of Education (www.save.org) and the American Foundation for Suicide Prevention (www.afsp.org). If there is a suicide hotline in your area, post the number for the kids to write down.

- School violence also has been a cause of teenage death in schools nationwide. You may want to talk about this as well, if you think it's appropriate for your group in your town. Ask your kids what causes teenagers to lash out in violence. Have they seen or experienced situations of school violence? What can your kids do to put an end to school violence and make their own schools safer? For more information, check out the Youth Specialties Web page (www.YouthSpecialties.com) for links and information, including www.disciples.org/violence.htm and Bulletproof? A Student Violence Prevention Program by Neighbors Who Care (www.neighborswhocare.org).

FRIENDS

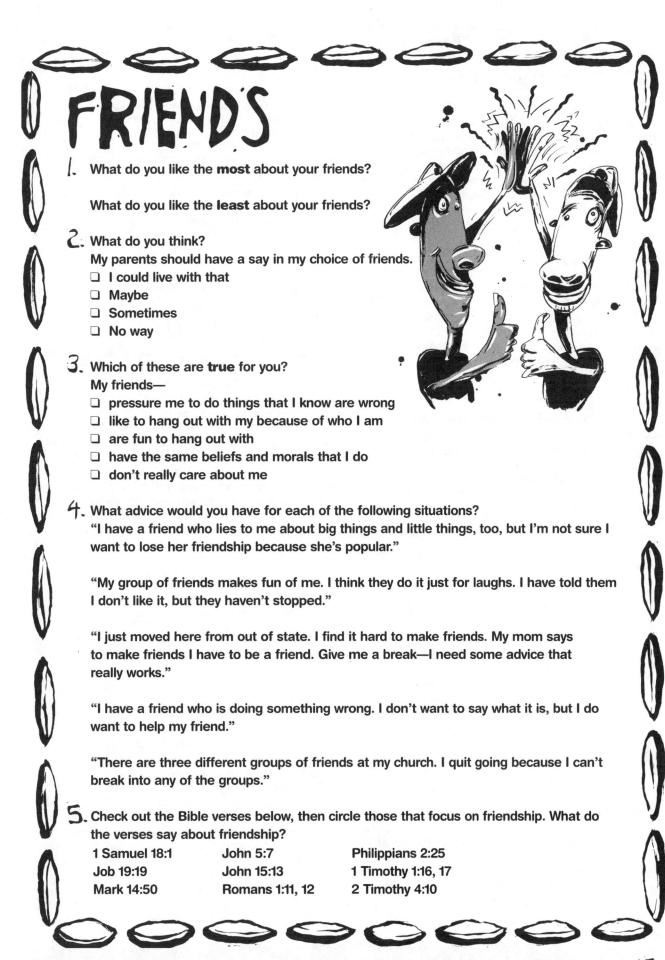

1. What do you like the **most** about your friends?

   What do you like the **least** about your friends?

2. What do you think?
   My parents should have a say in my choice of friends.
   - ❏ I could live with that
   - ❏ Maybe
   - ❏ Sometimes
   - ❏ No way

3. Which of these are **true** for you?
   My friends—
   - ❏ pressure me to do things that I know are wrong
   - ❏ like to hang out with my because of who I am
   - ❏ are fun to hang out with
   - ❏ have the same beliefs and morals that I do
   - ❏ don't really care about me

4. What advice would you have for each of the following situations?
   "I have a friend who lies to me about big things and little things, too, but I'm not sure I want to lose her friendship because she's popular."

   "My group of friends makes fun of me. I think they do it just for laughs. I have told them I don't like it, but they haven't stopped."

   "I just moved here from out of state. I find it hard to make friends. My mom says to make friends I have to be a friend. Give me a break—I need some advice that really works."

   "I have a friend who is doing something wrong. I don't want to say what it is, but I do want to help my friend."

   "There are three different groups of friends at my church. I quit going because I can't break into any of the groups."

5. Check out the Bible verses below, then circle those that focus on friendship. What do the verses say about friendship?

1 Samuel 18:1	John 5:7	Philippians 2:25
Job 19:19	John 15:13	1 Timothy 1:16, 17
Mark 14:50	Romans 1:11, 12	2 Timothy 4:10

FRIENDS [f r i e n d s]

THIS WEEK

Friendships are vital for teenagers. Because a family can only go so far in providing for the needs of kids, young teens crave friendships. And since friends teach each other so much, the friendships they establish can literally make or break their adolescent years. The TalkSheet discusses the importance of friendships and the influences that friends have on each other—both positive and negative.

OPENER

Start by asking your group to think of all the TV shows where they've seen friendships—there will be a ton of these, since almost every TV show revolves around friendships and relationships. Make a list of these shows and how friendship is portrayed. What have your kids learned about friendship from these shows? What makes these shows successful? What is the difference between opposite and same-sex friendships? Why do the characters value each other as friends? How have these friendships been abused or damaged?

How well do your group members know each other? Are they friends among themselves? Whether they are or not, encourage them to get to know each other better! Have each person in your group write two things (or more) about themselves on a piece of paper. Then collect all the papers and read each one aloud to the group. See if your group can guess who the person is based on the facts given. What was surprising about some of the facts given? What did your kids know or not know about each other? Who had an extra unique fact that no one knew? What keeps your kids from getting to know each other better?

THE DISCUSSION, BY NUMBERS

1. Create a master list of likes and dislikes, then circle those qualities that are mentioned more than once. What can your kids do about the qualities they like the least? Does everyone have these characteristics or are they unique among some people? Are they things that can be overlooked? Should they be overlooked?

2. Some kids get defensive when friends and parents are mentioned in the same sentence! You might get a variety of responses, but most will say that their parents shouldn't have a say. How can your kids choose their own friendships and still communicate with their parents? How are they going to handle their parents' disapproval of certain friends?

3. What are the reasons for their responses? Based on these questions, how do they treat their

friends? How do their friends treat them? How often do they influence their friends to do the wrong things? What is important to have good friendships?

4. You may want to pass out 3x5 cards and let the kids write their own answers, then read them as a group. Or create a discussion among the group. How would they handle these situations? What advice would they have? Is this advice good or bad? Why or why not?

5. What do these verses say about friendship? Ask the group to identify some of the characteristics of friendship found in the verses. Why do they think God created friendship?

THE CLOSE

You may want to wrap things up by talking about the important aspects of friendships. Point out that to *have* friends, you've got to *be* a friend. And emphasize healthy friendships versus unhealthy friendships. Do their friends pressure them into doing drugs? Drinking? Being sexually active? Challenge your kids to choose friends who build them up and encourage them to be their best—friendship is about supporting and caring for each other for who they are. Jesus is an example of a loyal, loving friend—he cared for his disciples and cares for each person today. How close are your kids to their forever Friend? What can your kids do to be better friends to others and to be a better friend with God?

MORE

● You may want to have your group take a look at biblical friendships. A few examples include David and Jonathan (1 Samuel 18 and 19), Jesus and Lazarus (John 11), Moses and God (Exodus 33), and Paul and Barnabas (Acts 14). What makes these friendships good? What qualities of friendship were shown? Are these still important today? Why or why not? What can your kids learn from these friendships? What other examples of friendship in the Bible can they find?

● It's important to have friends both inside and outside the church. How close is your group? How could your group grow closer to each other? Consider planning a special event for your kids to let them get to know each other better—a service project, a night to hang out and do something fun, or a weekly lunch at school with you. Or form an e-mail distribution list with your group and keep each other up to date on what's going on within the group, including sharing prayer requests, questions, and concerns.

THE GENESIS 1 QUESTION

1. Have you ever wondered if God really did create the heavens and the earth? Why or why not?

2. Which statements below do you think are **true**?
   - ❑ Science will prove the Bible to be wrong.
   - ❑ There's no way that people came from monkeys.
   - ❑ I have no doubt that God created the earth.
   - ❑ Maybe God used evolution as a way to create the earth.
   - ❑ If the Bible says it, then it's true.
   - ❑ God created me—and he created everything else, too.

3. Do you think a person can be a **Christian** and still believe in **evolution**?

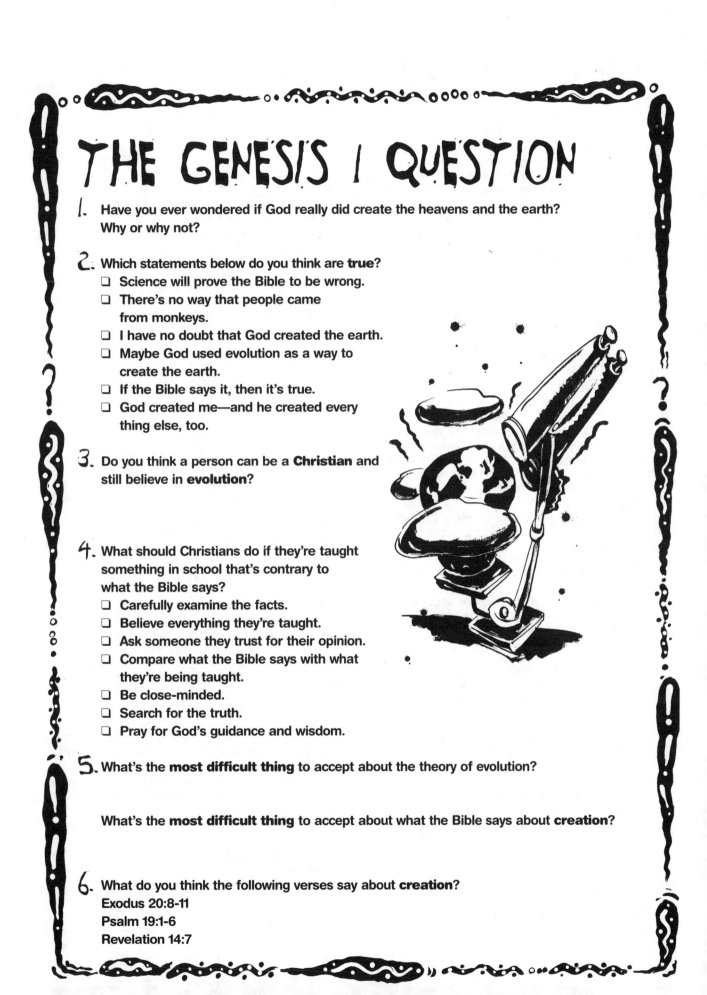

4. What should Christians do if they're taught something in school that's contrary to what the Bible says?
   - ❑ Carefully examine the facts.
   - ❑ Believe everything they're taught.
   - ❑ Ask someone they trust for their opinion.
   - ❑ Compare what the Bible says with what they're being taught.
   - ❑ Be close-minded.
   - ❑ Search for the truth.
   - ❑ Pray for God's guidance and wisdom.

5. What's the **most difficult thing** to accept about the theory of evolution?

   What's the **most difficult thing** to accept about what the Bible says about **creation**?

6. What do you think the following verses say about **creation**?
   Exodus 20:8-11
   Psalm 19:1-6
   Revelation 14:7

THE GENESIS 1 QUESTION [science and creation]

THIS WEEK

Teenagers, depending on where they go to school and who their teachers are, are hearing different stories about how the world was created, whether by evolution, the Big Bang theory, or other ideas. Your kids may be confronted with questions and doubts about the Bible's teachings and their religious upbringing—Christianity most likely conflicts with what they're learning in their science classes.

This may be a sensitive topic in some churches. It's important that you are familiar with the group's beliefs before starting this discussion.

OPENER

You may want to start by bringing in a toy, a large rock, a vegetable or fruit, and maybe a few other items to set before the group. Ask the group to describe how these things came into existence. Point out that it's easy for them to see that someone had to create the toy—but don't believe that God had to make the rock or grow the fruit!

Or show a video on creation or evolution—or bring some articles, facts, or information to discuss with your group. Check out these Internet resources—the Creation Research Society (www.creationresearch.org), Answers in Genesis Ministries International (www.answersingenesis.org), Christian Answers Network (www.christiananswers.net).

THE DISCUSSION, BY NUMBERS

1. What questions do your kids have about creation? How about evolution? What have they discussed in school or in church that has made them think about creation versus evolution?

2. How did your kids respond to these statements? Do your kids agree with each other? Why or why not? You may want to point out that science can never really prove the Bible wrong because science isn't 100 percent true either—in science, what is thought to be true one day gets thrown out when new data is analyzed.

3. Tough one, huh? Unfortunately this has been a litmus test for some Christians. Some Christians think that God may have used evolution as part of creation. The Bible is clear that God created the heavens and the earth—why question that?

4. How would your kids realistically handle these situations? How can they back their beliefs up when science speaks strongly for evolution? You may want brainstorm with the group additional ideas for handling difficult situations.

5. Your kids may have questions—that's okay. They're in the midst of learning a lot, taking in information, and forming their own opinions. Give them the chance to share their doubts—but encourage them in their faith. You may want to point out your own beliefs or doubts that you've had in the past. What does God think of doubting? What can they do if they start to question God?

6. Read each of the passages and some kids to share what they wrote or thought about the verses. You may want to make a list of the words that describe God's miracle of creation.

THE CLOSE

Point out that God is involved in creation—in its beginning, sustenance, and end. He still is creating today—new people, plants, animals, and more! Scientists are still learning new things about the earth and the species on it.

You may want to point out the awesomeness of God's creation. What have your kids experienced that has put them at awe? A sunset? A sunrise? A new litter of puppies? A new baby brother or sister? Point out that nature shows God's power and involvement in creation. King David wrote many psalms on God's creation and nature—you may want to close by reading Psalm 100.

MORE

● Ask each of your kids to find two facts either for evolution or creation. Encourage them to search the Internet, check out their science textbooks at school, or ask their teacher. What information did they find? How does this information compare with the biblical account of creation? How believable is this information? Why or why not? How have their beliefs been shaped from this discussion?

● If you have someone available, you may want to invite a science teacher, professor, or researcher to come into your meeting for discussion. Allow your students to ask questions, but to listen carefully. Be careful to mediate the Q&A—don't allow your kids to disrespect or challenge the interviewee, especially if he or she is an evolutionist. Your goal is to challenge the thinking of your kids and not to disrespect the beliefs of the other person.

INTO ALL THE WORLD

1. **Have you ever thought about being a missionary?**
   - ❏ **Never**
   - ❏ **Many times**
   - ❏ **One time**
   - ❏ **Several times**
   - ❏ **It is what I want to do**

2. **Suppose God wrote a want ad to be placed in your church bulletin, asking for missionaries. What might the insert say? Complete each of the following sentences with your ideas.**

   > Wanted: Christian Missionaries!
   > You will need to know—
   > You must want to—
   > It would be nice if—
   > You must be able to—

3. **Put an arrow ⇨ by three things you'd like our group to do.**
   Pray regularly for a specific missionary.
   Write letters to a missionary.
   Have a Bible study about missions and missionaries.
   Go on a missions trip.
   Work on a missions project each month.
   Watch a video about missions.
   Send money or materials to a missionary.
   Find out what our church's missions program is doing.

4. **How do you think about the following statements—do you A (agree) or D (disagree)?**
   ___ **You must be a super-spiritual person to be a missionary.**
   ___ **God's favorite work is missionary work.**
   ___ **Only churchy nerds become missionaries.**
   ___ **It's an honor to serve Christ as a missionary.**
   ___ **Most people in today's world are already Christians.**
   ___ **Our church already does enough missions stuff.**

5. **Read Acts 1:8. If you're a Christian, how will you change your life to live for this cause you've been called to?**

From *More Junior High-Middle School TalkSheets—Updated!* by David Lynn. Permission to reproduce this page granted only for use in the buyer's own youth group. www.YouthSpecialties.com

49

INTO ALL THE WORLD [foreign missions]

THIS WEEK

The youth in your church may hear exciting adventure stories about missionaries, see pictures or videos, and pray for missionaries—but do they picture themselves being missionaries? This TalkSheet will open up a discussion on foreign missions and help them understand their part in taking the life-changing message of Jesus Christ to all the world.

OPENER

You may want to start this discussion by asking your group a few questions—

- What do your kids think missionaries are? Christians living in the jungle learning unknown languages? Those spreading the gospel to the starving people in Africa? People in the inner city reaching out to drug addicts and prostitutes?
- What do missionaries do besides telling the news of Jesus Christ?
- How are missionaries supported? Where do they get their money, clothes, and other necessities?
- In what regions of the world are there missionaries? What would be the most dangerous place to be?

Your kids may have many different ideas of missions work, based on what they've seen or heard in church or experienced in their own lives. Before this session you may want to find information on several different ministries. There are hundreds of ministries that reach out to people of all ages in nearly all regions of the world. For links to these organizations, check out www.gospelcom.net and browse under the category *missions*. Point out some of these organizations to your group, including what these missionaries do, where, for what ages, and for what purpose. Also, point out that some missionaries are supported by churches and may not have information on the Internet. Be sure to get some information on the missionaries that your church supports. Where are these missionaries and how long have they been there?

Point out that missionaries just aren't overseas in the most remote areas of the world—they're in countries and cities worldwide, reaching out in the name of Christ. Some work with children, teenagers, families, prisoners, military people, and more. Some are life long missionaries and some aren't. God has called these people into unique ministries, depending on their skills and gifts. And some do other stuff besides teaching about God—some are doctors, nurses, teachers, counselors, or pastors. Some build houses, cook food, teach classes, translate languages, and more.

THE DISCUSSION, BY NUMBERS

1. Ask some in your group to share their opinions. How do they think it might be like to be a missionary? What would an average day be like? How do missionaries have fun? Do missionaries sin? What other questions do your group members have about missionaries?

2. What did your kids write for each? You may want to create a master list with your group.

3. How do your kids feel about getting involved in missions? You may want to wait until you wrap up the discussion before challenging the group to get involved.

4. Consider each of the statements and how they apply to winning the world for Christ. How did your kids react to these statements? Did they agree or disagree? Why or why not?

5. How do your kids think Acts 1:8 can be lived out in junior high or middle school? How can they start to reach out in their school, to their friends, teachers, coaches, and classmates?

THE CLOSE

How can your kids get involved in missionary work? You may want to read the Great Commission found in Matthew 28:18-20—God has called everyone to reach out! Challenge your kids to think about they can work as agent for Christ today, in their own lives, and in the future. And encourage them to pray for the missionaries worldwide. You may want to close by talking about what you can do as a group to reach out and plan a missions project or reach out.

MORE

- What questions do your kids have about missions and missionaries? Encourage them to write these questions down and send these via letter or e-mail to several of the missionaries that your church supports. Be sure to read the responses when you receive them and to pray for these missionaries with your group.
- Consider hosting a fundraiser for the missionaries in your church, such as a special dinner, dessert night, clothing drive, or other event. Get your kids involved in the planning—and be sure to let the congregation know the purpose of the fundraiser! You may want to check with your church missions committee to see if there is anything in particular that certain missionaries need, such as books, clothing, school supplies, and Bibles. Possibly use the money raised to buy materials for these missionaries.

PARENT'S VS. PEERS

1. Do you **agree** with this statement? Why or why not?
   Most teenagers rebel against their parents or guardians.

2. If you had a life-changing decision to make, would you most likely go to your parents or to your friends for advice?

   Why?

3. Who would you go to for advice on the following—**P (parents)** or **F (friends)**?
   ___ if you had a problem with a friend
   ___ if you felt bad about something you had done wrong
   ___ if you had concerns about sex
   ___ if you wondered what clothes to buy
   ___ if you had a problem at school
   ___ if you were contemplating suicide
   ___ if you were offered drugs or alcohol
   ___ if you had questions about God
   ___ if you had doubts about the future
   ___ if you were struggling with your grades

4. On the line below, indicate with an **X** who has the most influence on you— parents or friends.

   Parents   **Friends**

5. Check out these verses and decide if each one is an example of a friend being a **good** or **bad** influence?

Genesis 13:12, 13	Psalm 1:1, 2
Genesis 13:18	Psalm 1:4, 5
2 Kings 17:28	Proverbs 1:7-9
2 Kings 17:34	Proverbs 1:10-16

PARENTS VS. PEERS [influence of parents and friends]

THIS WEEK

Parents are still the biggest influence on junior highers and middle schoolers—but at this age peer groups are becoming more and more important. One of your responsibilities as a youth leader is to affirm the role of parents while at the same time helping kids live in the world of their peers. This TalkSheet will give you a chance to talk about the role of parents and peers in the lives of the teeenagers.

Be sensitive to some of your group members who may not have good relationships with their parents, come from broken homes, or live with grandparents or other guardians.

OPENER

To start this discussion, place two chairs facing each other in the front or the middle of the room. Print the word *parent* on a paper and tape it to one of the chairs. Put the word *peer* on another chair. Then you can either ask for volunteers to come up and take turns sitting in the chairs—or let your kids take turns coming up to sit in the chairs.

Tell your kids that each chair represents either a parent or a peer perspective—they could be the same or different, depending on the issue. Give the volunteers a topic to debate from both a parent and a peer viewpoint. These topics could include dating, allowance, bad grades, curfew, getting grounded, church attendance, homework, music, and chores. The person who sits in each chair should take either a parent or a peer point of view.

How did this activity affect how your kids think about parents and peers? Was it hard to think like a parent? Why or why not? What's easier to defend as—a parent or a peer? Why or why not? Use these questions to springboard into this discussion on parents versus peers.

THE DISCUSSION, BY NUMBERS

1. Point out that being a teenager doesn't mean one has to rebel. Why do some kids rebel more than others? What makes kids rebel? Is it good for family relationships? Why or why not?

2. Who do your kids go to for advice? Ask them how they decide who to go to with their problems. Who are the more influential—parents or peers?

3. This is a follow-up to question 2 and is a barometer of your kids' relationships with their parents. It's normal for some junior highers or middle schoolers to feel more comfortable talking about certain things with their peers.

4. Where did your kids put the mark on the line? Do they think it's bad to be influenced more by parents or peers? Point out that parents do need to have a place in their lives—and youth need their parents, too.

5. Place the headings good influence and bad influence on a whiteboard or poster board. As the group shares responses to the verses, put the verses under the appropriate heading. How were these characters good or bad influences? Why or why not? What did your kids learn from this activity?

THE CLOSE

Kids today live in two different worlds—one with parents and one with friends, both who have different expectations and demands from them. God isn't against friends (or parents). But he has offered some guidelines in the Bible related to influences. You may want to read Proverbs 1:8-19—this is only one guideline that must be balanced with others. It's important to rely on the adults in your kids' lives and to honor them—and to balance your relationship with both parents and peers. What can your kids do to balance parents and friends? How can your kids get closer to their parents?

MORE

● How does the media influence how your kids think of parents versus peers? Ask your kids a few of these questions and see how they respond—
⇨ Are most TV shows pro-parent or pro-peer?
⇨ Who do magazines (like *Teen* or *YM*) emphasize more—parents or peers? How?
⇨ What movies have you seen lately that promote parental or peer relationships?
⇨ How about advertisements? Do your kids normally see advertisements for kids with parents or peers in them?

What conclusions can your group make based on the media? Is your society pro-parent or pro-peer? How do these influence your kids' relation ships with parents and peers?

● You may want to plan an event or meeting with your kids and their parents or guardians. Or have your kids talk about one issue with their parents this week. Challenge them to take one topic or situation from the intro and ask their parents about. Did their parents handle it the same way the group did in the intro? Why or why not? What other input did their parents have? Do your group members feel differently about their parents?

IT'S YOUR CALL

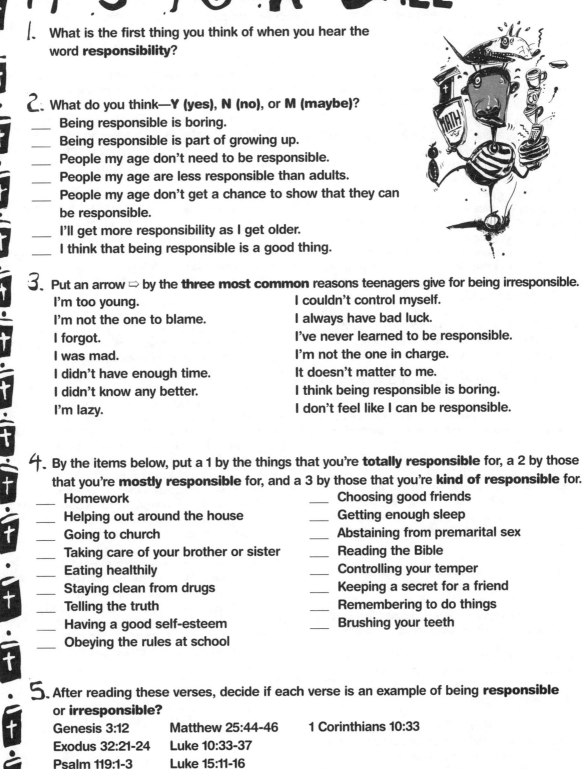

1. What is the first thing you think of when you hear the word **responsibility**?

2. What do you think—**Y (yes), N (no)**, or **M (maybe)**?
   ___ Being responsible is boring.
   ___ Being responsible is part of growing up.
   ___ People my age don't need to be responsible.
   ___ People my age are less responsible than adults.
   ___ People my age don't get a chance to show that they can be responsible.
   ___ I'll get more responsibility as I get older.
   ___ I think that being responsible is a good thing.

3. Put an arrow ⇨ by the **three most common** reasons teenagers give for being irresponsible.

   I'm too young.   I couldn't control myself.
   I'm not the one to blame.   I always have bad luck.
   I forgot.   I've never learned to be responsible.
   I was mad.   I'm not the one in charge.
   I didn't have enough time.   It doesn't matter to me.
   I didn't know any better.   I think being responsible is boring.
   I'm lazy.   I don't feel like I can be responsible.

4. By the items below, put a 1 by the things that you're **totally responsible** for, a 2 by those that you're **mostly responsible** for, and a 3 by those that you're **kind of responsible** for.
   ___ Homework   ___ Choosing good friends
   ___ Helping out around the house   ___ Getting enough sleep
   ___ Going to church   ___ Abstaining from premarital sex
   ___ Taking care of your brother or sister ___ Reading the Bible
   ___ Eating healthily   ___ Controlling your temper
   ___ Staying clean from drugs   ___ Keeping a secret for a friend
   ___ Telling the truth   ___ Remembering to do things
   ___ Having a good self-esteem   ___ Brushing your teeth
   ___ Obeying the rules at school

5. After reading these verses, decide if each verse is an example of being **responsible** or **irresponsible**?
   Genesis 3:12   Matthew 25:44-46   1 Corinthians 10:33
   Exodus 32:21-24   Luke 10:33-37
   Psalm 119:1-3   Luke 15:11-16

IT'S YOUR CALL [r e s p o n s i b i l i t y]

THIS WEEK

Responsibility—young teens say they can handle it. Adults question what teenagers do with it. How much responsibility is good for junior highers and middle schoolers? And how do your kids handle it? Responsibility is an important growing-up issue can be discussed using this TalkSheet.

OPENER

You may want to start off by making a master list of all the responsibilities that the kids in your group have. This may be a long list, depending on your group. Some responsibilities include homework, personal hygiene, babysitting, helping out around the house, getting to and from school safely, being honest with their parents, things like that. Then on a scale of 1-10 (10 being very responsible), how would your kids rate themselves for each responsibility?

You may want to have them right down their answers anonymously, or ask how responsible peers their age, in general, are. Why is it easier to be responsible at some times than others? What is the hardest part about being responsible? What responsibilities do your kids have now that they didn't have before? List some responsibilities that your kids will have as they get older. What role do their parents, teachers, or other adults have in the amount of responsibility that your kids have?

THE DISCUSSION, BY NUMBERS

1. What does the word *responsibility* mean to your kids? With the group, come up with a definition of responsibility.

2. Ask your kids to share their opinions about responsibility. Some junior highers or middle schoolers want to be responsible sometimes, but they don't want all the responsibility. What's wrong with this thinking? How is trust involved in responsibility?

3. Which of these excuses have your kids heard? You may want to talk about why so many people—not just teenagers—act irresponsibly. How does this hurt relationships with parents and friends? How can being irresponsible impact the future?

4. This is a spin-off from the intro—why do your kids act responsibly in the areas they circled? What would happen if they didn't take responsibility for these things?

5. What did your kids learn about responsibility from these verses? Point out that being responsible hasn't changed over time—people have always been held responsible and always will be!

THE CLOSE

Point out that the human nature is sinful—people like blaming others rather than taking responsibility. The "it's not my fault" thinking began in the garden with Adam and Eve—and it continues today! How can your kids balance their responsibilities with the view of their parents? Teachers? Coaches? Other adults?

Adults are concerned about irresponsibility because they're concerned about their teenagers. But teenagers see responsibility differently than adults. Most teenagers think they are acting responsibly with respect to their future—their "future" being tomorrow or tonight. Teenagers also think that responsibility is equal to growing up, but they've confused responsibility with maturity.

Close by pointing out that responsibility is a privilege—if your kids abuse their responsibilities, they'll most likely be punished somehow, either by parents, teachers, police, and so on. Challenge your kids to honor their responsibilities and to start making wise choices for the future.

MORE

● You may want to ask parents, pastor, and some other adults to attend a panel for a Q&A with your students. Encourage your kids to ask questions and vice versa—how do adults know how much responsibility is right? How is trust involved in responsibility? What are the consequences for not being responsible? If you don't want to do a panel, encourage your kids to ask three adults questions on responsibility this week—challenge them to ask their teachers, coaches, parents, employers, and anyone else who hold them responsible.

● Give your kids responsibility and see how they follow through! A few suggestions include putting your kids in charge of next week's meeting, having them work together to plan an event or fundraiser, helping out the pastor plan a church service, and so on. But don't make this a burden! You can make this as fun as you want. And you can either do this before the meeting or after it—then talk about the responsibility later. How did they feel having these responsibilities? What did they like about it? What didn't they like? How do responsibilities now prepare them for future responsibilities?

THE BLURRING OF MORALITY ?

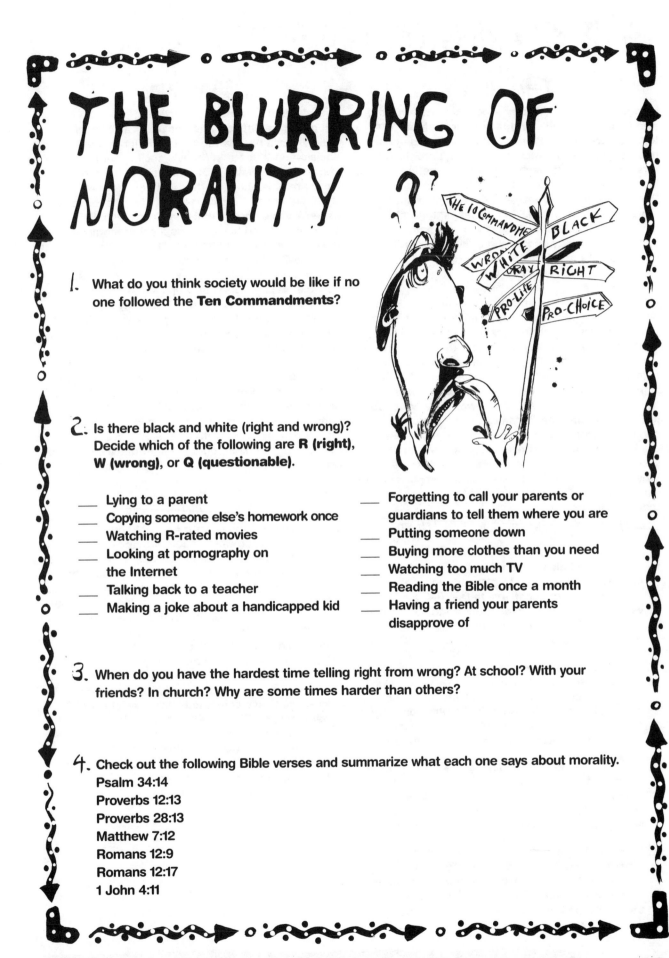

1. What do you think society would be like if no one followed the **Ten Commandments**?

2. Is there black and white (right and wrong)? Decide which of the following are **R (right)**, **W (wrong)**, or **Q (questionable)**.

___ Lying to a parent
___ Copying someone else's homework once
___ Watching R-rated movies
___ Looking at pornography on the Internet
___ Talking back to a teacher
___ Making a joke about a handicapped kid

___ Forgetting to call your parents or guardians to tell them where you are
___ Putting someone down
___ Buying more clothes than you need
___ Watching too much TV
___ Reading the Bible once a month
___ Having a friend your parents disapprove of

3. When do you have the hardest time telling right from wrong? At school? With your friends? In church? Why are some times harder than others?

4. Check out the following Bible verses and summarize what each one says about morality.
   Psalm 34:14
   Proverbs 12:13
   Proverbs 28:13
   Matthew 7:12
   Romans 12:9
   Romans 12:17
   1 John 4:11

THE BLURRING OF MORALITY [m o r a l i t y]

THIS WEEK

Morality. What is it? And how do your kids form their own ideas of morality and their set of values? In today's society, what's right and what's wrong has been distorted—the media, teachers, parents, pastors, and peers all teach your kids competing values. Morality today is no longer just black or white. Because of that, parents and the church must be more intentional in teaching values and moral standards. This TalkSheet will give you an opportunity to talk about morality and how your kids interpret values in today's society.

OPENER

How well do your kids know the Ten Commandments? For this intro you'll need a large poster board or white board. Ask your group to think of as many of the Ten Commandments as they can. See if they can remember the order of the Ten Commandments, too. Then take turns reading each command from Exodus 20 with your group. After each commandment is read, ask your group to put it in their own words. What does it mean to them today? Make a master list of all the commandments written in their own words. Then ask the kids how and why these commands still apply to people today. Are some more important than others? Why or why not? Which one is the most important and why? How can your kids follow these commands in their own lives?

THE DISCUSSION, BY NUMBERS

1. Why did God give us commandments? Were commandments given to make life miserable or to show them the best way to live life? Explore why more and more people are living contrary to God's way and the present and future consequences of doing so.

2. These situations force kids into making moral choices. Have them describe how they decided what was right and what was wrong. Were God's standards reflected in their decisions? Which ones were questionable? How can people decide between right and wrong when there's no clear answers?

3. You may want to take the time to talk about peer pressure and its influence on individual morality (see Parents vs. Peers on page 51). When do your kids struggle with morality? Why is it hard to decide what's right and wrong?

4. Each of the passages contains a command from God. Talk about how God's morality—if lived out—is better than the world's morality. Point out that God's command are boundaries to keep them safe and protect their hearts from sin.

THE CLOSE

There's no doubt that the decisions your kids face will get more difficult and uncertain as they grow older. They'll need a moral foundation to base their decision on. People in today's society set their own standards and values. Standards that were once clear are now blurred—they've become gray.

Point out that it's hard to stick to a set of values, especially in a society that questions them. Remind the kids that God has given us a set of morals in the Bible—he's laid out clear boundaries. You may want to read the Ten Commandments with your group again, or look back at the set you wrote in the intro. Review how the group decided they applied today even though they were written thousands of years ago.

What other rules does God give in the Bible? What other commands did Jesus give in the New Testament? What benefits come from following God's rules and living for him?

Close by reminding your kids that God forgives and forgets. No one will ever be able to follow God's laws perfectly—that's part of being human. But if someone loves God, they'll follow what he says is best for them. Close with a time of prayer and encourage your kids to start following God's boundaries and asking God for wisdom and guidance in their decisions.

MORE

- You may want to ask your kids to keep track of how many of the Ten Commandments are broken in the next TV show or movie they watch. Have them note what the movie was rated and what it was about. Follow up with your kids to talk about morals in the media. How common is it for your kids to see murder, adultery, or swearing in the shows they see? What impact does this have on how people live and treat each other? What can your kids do to set boundaries around themselves?
- What analogies can your kids make between God's commands and boundaries for their lives? How are God's commands like a safety net? A parachute? A life jacket? What would life be like with out these rules to keep them on track? Make a list of all the analogies that your kids can make. Then talk about how each one explains the importance of God's commands.

BUY NOW, PAY LATER

1. How would you finish this statement?
   Compared with most other people at my school, I have—
   - ❏ Better stuff than they do
   - ❏ About the same amount of stuff they do
   - ❏ About the same kind of stuff as they do
   - ❏ More clothes and stuff than they do
   - ❏ Not as much good stuff as they do
   - ❏ Less clothes and stuff than they do

2. Circle the things that you think kids your age should be able to have.

Big-screen television	Computer
Pager	Jet ski or snowmobile
Credit card	High-quality bicycle
Cellular telephone	Video game equipment
Motor scooter	VCR or DVD player
Latest style clothing	CD player
Latest style shoes	Other—
Sports equipment	

   Cross out the things that you personally own and put a star ☆ by the things you'd like to have by the time you graduate from high school.

3. If you were given a lot of money today (like thousands of dollars), what would you do with it?

4. What do you think—do you **A (agree)** or **D (disagree)**?
   ___ A person can have too many possessions.
   ___ The more people get, the less they want.
   ___ There's too much emphasis on money and buying stuff.
   ___ There's nothing wrong with buying things you can't yet afford.
   ___ Owning too many material possessions makes it difficult to be a Christian.
   ___ Material things can make a person popular.
   ___ People can buy anything they want as long as they have a credit card.
   ___ Having enough money is the number one priority for grown-ups.
   ___ Advertisements make me want to buy more than I need.

5. Check out the following verses and write what you think each has to say about **money** and **possessions**.

Exodus 20:17	Luke 12:15
Matthew 6:24	Luke 14:33

BUY NOW, PAY LATER [materialism and consumerism]

THIS WEEK

There's no doubt that consumerism has infected our society—and affected the youth culture as well. The media has influenced the expectations of young people, whether they're poor, middle class, or rich. Teens between the ages of 12-17 spend over $100 billion annually—that's over $4,400 each*! And with the anticipated growth of the teen population by the year 2007, consumerism by this age will continue to boom. Is this consumerism acceptable by Christian standards? And how do your churched kids handle their money with a mentality surrounding them that says they need it all? This TalkSheet explores the topic of possessions and materialistic values and how your kids can avoid getting caught in the urge to buy now, pay later.

OPENER

Bring in a stack of ads from the Sunday paper, some magazines with advertisements, or some catalogs. Break the your group into clusters and ask them to cut out stuff from the ads that they personally own and stuff that they want to have. Then have them make two stacks of the cut-out ads—things they have, and things they want. Ask the groups to compare which stack is bigger. Do they *need* the stuff they want? Why or why not?

Or give each person a piece of paper and something to write with, then have them make a list of all the stuff they have right now. That's everything they wearing, plus what's in their wallets, pockets, and purses. Have them include things like glasses, contact lenses, and braces. Next to each item they should write down an estimate of how much each item costs to calculate the total worth of what they're wearing. Then add up the individual totals and write down the total for the whole group. Point out that this amount could be more than the annual income of families in third-world countries. Pretty scary, huh?

THE DISCUSSION, BY NUMBERS

1. Ask your kids how often they compare themselves to others. Why is there so much pressure to have the right clothes or other stuff? How much of this stuff is actually necessary? Why or why not? How might your kids think differently about money and possessions if they didn't compare themselves to others?

2. What items does your group think kids their age should be able to own? Is it necessary for them to have any of these? Why or why not?

3. What would your kids do with their money? What do they think teenagers in general would do with this money? Discuss the different priorities that your kids may have.

4. Take a vote and debate each of these statements. You may want to split your kids into groups and ask them to back up their opinions with Bible verses.

5. These passages should challenge your students to think about their perspective on possessions. You may want to divide them into small groups and ask them to discuss a Christian view of possessions and materialism in light of the passages.

THE CLOSE

Sometimes it's hard to avoid getting caught up in materialism and consumerism, especially when society is absorbed in advertisements, commercials, and the urge to buy. Christ warned his disciples and others about the danger of coveting. Getting caught up in materialism gets in the way of living life—and living for God.

Point out to the group that comparing themselves to others will make them discontented and unhappy. And wanting things that you can't have or afford only makes you unhappy. Jesus warned that possessions won't provide happiness—only God can fill people with joy and contentment. You may want to read the parable of the sower (Matthew 13:1-23) and close with a time of prayer, asking God to guide decisions and to fill your group with contentment from *him*—not from possessions or money.

MORE

● Consider doing a fundraiser, clothing drive, food drive, or some other activity to help a charity or other organization. You may want to plan a garage sale or church rummage sale for people to sell those things that they don't want or need. Then donate the money and leftover items.

● How do advertisements affect materialism and consumerism? Ask your kids to make a list of everywhere they see advertisements—on clothing, on buses, on the Internet, and even on cereal boxes. Where do they see advertising? How does advertising influence people to buy things they don't need? How can your kids keep advertisements from getting to them?

---

* Teen Fact Book 2000, Channel One Network: New York, Los Angeles, Chicago. Used by permission.

THINK IT THROUGH

1. What are **three problems** that kids your age face?

2. Do you **A (agree)** or **D (disagree)** with the statements below?

   ___ It's easier for Christians to solve their problems than it is for people who aren't Christians.

   ___ Christian teenagers have more problems than those who aren't Christians.

   ___ Adults don't understand the problems that young people face today.

   ___ God cares about only the big problems in my life, not the little ones.

   ___ I have adults in my life that I can talk to about problems I face.

   ___ Young people must find their own solutions to the problems they encounter in life.

3. Which is true for you?
   My Christian beliefs help me make the right choice when I face a problem.
   ❑ All of the time
   ❑ Most of the time
   ❑ Some of the time
   ❑ None of the time

4. Read the following verses—what do you think each has to say about **solving problems**?
   Psalm 34:19

   Psalm 120:1

   Romans 8:28

   James 1:2-5

THINK IT THROUGH [problem solving]

THIS WEEK

Some junior highers and middle schoolers freeze when they face new or big problems. Most aren't sure where to turn or what to do. This TalkSheet provides the opportunity to discuss different perspectives on problem solving and how a Christian young person can handle them.

Be aware that some kids in your group may be dealing with problems in their lives—drug use, alcoholism, premarital sex, depression, physical or sexual abuse, divorce at home, pornography, and more.

OPENER

Before you start, write some case scenario problems on pieces of paper. A few examples include—
* You're just not doing well in your classes and your parents are angry. But you're trying your hardest.
* Alana started dating Caleb two months ago and he wants to have sex. But she's not sure.
* Jordan's mom was diagnosed with cancer. She may live only a few months.
* You've found out that your closest friend has started smoking cigarettes.
* Josh got cut from the basketball team and now his so-called friends on the team have ditched him.
* Lorna just isn't fitting in at school—she's tried to dress cool, be nice, and all that. But it hasn't worked.
* Andres came home on Friday to find his parents screaming at each other. They've been fighting a lot.

Feel free to expand on these, leave any out, or add any that you think of—these are to help you get started.

Split your kids into groups and give each group a problem. Then ask them to read the problem and think about how they would handle the situation—realistically. What would the implications be if they made different decisions? How easy is it to find solutions to these problems? Are these realistic teenage problems or not? How often have your kids heard of situations like these? Use this activity to launch into your TalkSheet discussion and keep these thoughts alive throughout the discussion.

THE DISCUSSION, BY NUMBERS

1. Make a master list of all problems—then ask which ones your kids think are the worst. Why do they think these problems are so common? What are the top three problems of kids their age? Are these problems that will go away as they grow up or not?

2. Ask your kids to say whether they disagreed or agreed. Talk about the differing opinions and encourage your group members to explain why they agree or disagree. Be prepared to give your own views in response to some of the questions, but be sure to let the kids sort out their answers first.

3. Use this question to discuss how Christians can incorporate their beliefs into their decision-making and problem solving. How big of a role do your kids' beliefs play in their decision-making? Why or why not?

4. Be sure to give opportunities for different kids to share their perspectives on the passages. How would God want young people to face the problems they encounter?

THE CLOSE

Remind your group that God is a partner in problem solving. Most Christians would probably agree that God and his people work together—he guides and enables them to solve the problems. Emphasize to your kids that God is able to help in solve problems. But they need to be willing to come to him with their problems and concerns and trust that he is able to handle them!

Some of your kids may be more sensitive to these issues than others. Encourage your kids to find a trusted adult to talk with—including you, if they feel comfortable. Stress that it's vital for them to get help in dealing with these problems.

MORE

● You may want to continue this discussion with a Q&A with your group. Ask your kids to write down problems they are struggling with (be sure to keep it anonymous). Then collect the problems and read them individually to the group. Be sure to screen them for appropriateness before you read them out loud. Then have your group to brainstorm solutions to the problems. What advice do they have for each other? How can God help in the situations? What are some tangible solutions for finding answers?

● What are some ways that that TV and movie characters deal with problems? You may want to show a clip of a TV show or movie and then talk with the group about how the character(s) handled their problems. What could they have done differently? Did they handle the situation effectively? Why or why not? What does advice does society have for dealing with problems? Are these healthy solutions or not?

SEEKING THE TRUTH

1. Answer the following questions by placing the letters (A, B, C, D, or E) where you think they fit on the line below.
   a. How many people at your school know their astrological signs?
   b. How many people at your school believe in powers like ESP, contact with the dead, visualization, or magic?
   c. How many people at your school wear crystals?
   d. How many people at your school practice or are fascinated with witchcraft?
   e. How many people at your school have called a psychic hotline?

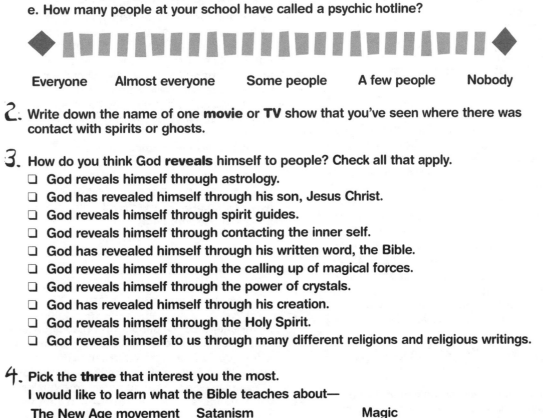

| Everyone | Almost everyone | Some people | A few people | Nobody |

2. Write down the name of one **movie** or **TV** show that you've seen where there was contact with spirits or ghosts.

3. How do you think God **reveals** himself to people? Check all that apply.
   ❑ God reveals himself through astrology.
   ❑ God has revealed himself through his son, Jesus Christ.
   ❑ God reveals himself through spirit guides.
   ❑ God reveals himself through contacting the inner self.
   ❑ God has revealed himself through his written word, the Bible.
   ❑ God reveals himself through the calling up of magical forces.
   ❑ God reveals himself through the power of crystals.
   ❑ God has revealed himself through his creation.
   ❑ God reveals himself through the Holy Spirit.
   ❑ God reveals himself to us through many different religions and religious writings.

4. Pick the **three** that interest you the most.
   I would like to learn what the Bible teaches about—

The New Age movement	Satanism	Magic
Reincarnation	Eastern mysticism	Tarot cards
Astrology	Crystal power	Channeling
Feng shui	Psychic hotlines	Other—
Witchcraft	The occult	

5. Take a look at **Deuteronomy 18:9-14**—what do you think God is teaching you from this passage?

SEEKING THE TRUTH [spiritual trends and false religions]

THIS WEEK

Many junior highers and middle schoolers have encountered crystals, psychics, horoscopes, witchcraft, false religions, and Eastern meditation techniques. The television, movies, the Internet, magazines, and music expose youth to these spiritual trends and false religions. This TalkSheet will give you an opportunity to talk about these spiritual counterfeits with your group.

Be sensitive to your group during this discussion. Some churches don't like to openly discuss these issues. And some of your kids may have been involved in this stuff—or have friends who are involved in these things.

OPENER

On a poster board or whiteboard, write down the following (and any others you'd like to include)—
* horoscopes
* Ouija boards
* tarot cards
* psychic hotlines
* dream discussions and analysis
* chants and deep meditation
* hypnosis
* palm reading

Ask your group if they know what each of these are. What does each one test or reveal? Do kids know people who are involved in using one or more of these? Are there any practices that aren't on the list? How reliable or powerful are these practices? How accurate are each of these for telling the truth?

Now hold up a Bible in front of your group. How does the Bible compare to the list above? Explain to your group that the Bible can be used to measure the truth of spiritual teachings and beliefs. And today there's so much counterfeit spiritual information, there needs to be a source of truth by which to gauge all other beliefs. The Bible is that source of truth—what you'll be talking about in this TalkSheet!

THE DISCUSSION, BY NUMBERS

1. This item will show you how much counterfeit spiritual activity is occurring at local schools. Take a poll of the group's responses. Ask the group why people would believe it is important to know their astrological signs. To believe in magic spiritual forces? To wear a crystal? To dabble in witchcraft? To trust a psychic?

2. Make a list of recent movies and TV shows with counterfeit spiritual content. Ask the group how these movies influence people in subtle and not-so-subtle ways.

3. The following are ways in which God reveals himself—through his son, Jesus Christ; through his written word, the Bible; through his creation; and through the Holy Spirit. What do your kid think about each of these? Do they know how to look for God?

4. Is your group interested in learning more about these counterfeit spiritual movements? If so, you may want to pursue one or more within a Christian context.

5. How does this passage apply to people today? What are the dangers of getting involved in false religious practices?

THE CLOSE

Looking for and wanting guidance is a normal part of life and growing up—especially for teenagers. Even the children of Israel continuously sought guidance—sometimes from God and other times from false gods and spiritual mediums. But God has promised to guide those who follow him (Psalm 31:3)—Christians have access to the infinite yet personal God of the Bible who's there all the time. You may want to close by reading Hebrews 13:9 and with a time of prayer.

For more information on the issues discussed, you may want to contact one of these organizations—Spiritual Counterfeit Projects (www.scp-inc.org), Christian Research Institute (www.equip.org), or the World Religions Index (http://wri.leaderu.com).

MORE

● You may want to ask your senior pastor or someone else who is familiar with other religions to come in and talk with your group. What questions do your kids have about these religions? What can Christians do for people who they know are involved in these trends and religions? Where can they go to find more information?

● The Bible is very clear about the power of Satan. You may want to spend some time talking about the dangers of getting involved in satanism and its practices, including meditation and other practices that are considered harmless by some. With your group, find and read some verses in the Bible that talk about the power of Satan and the spiritual battle with Christians. A few include 1 Peter 5:8, James 4:7, 2 Timothy 2:26, and Ephesians 6:10-17. What do these verses say to Christians? What warnings does it give? How can Christians resist the devil and stand firm?

WHO'S NUMBER ONE?

1. Do you think **A (agree)** or **D (disagree)** with these statements?
   ___ There are other important religions in the world.
   ___ It's easy to have idols that replace God.
   ___ Everybody has an idol of some kind.
   ___ Things like money could never replace God.
   ___ God doesn't love people who are into other religions.

2. Label each statement with **M (that's me)** or **N (that's not me)**.
   ___ I usually choose church activities over other activities when I'm busy.
   ___ I sometimes hide my Christianity from others so I won't be embarrassed.
   ___ I use my Christian beliefs when I make everyday decisions.
   ___ I have many friends who are also Christians.
   ___ I have a lot more to learn about how to apply my Christianity to my life.
   ___ I like talking with others about my Christian faith.
   ___ I am happy about being a Christian.

3. Look over your response to question 2, then answer the following question—
   How important is the influence of Christianity in your everyday life?
   ❏ The most important influence in my life
   ❏ One of a couple important things in my life
   ❏ Sort of an important influence in my life.
   ❏ Barely important in my life

4. How committed to Jesus Christ were each of the people described in these verses?
   Put a 1 by those that describe **total commitment**, a 2 by those that describe **mixed commitment**, and a 3 by those that **aren't really committed** at all.

Matthew 16:24	Luke 4:28, 29	John 7:5	John 12:42
Matthew 28:17	Luke 14:33	John 7:13	John 19:38

From *More Junior High-Middle School TalkSheets—Updated!* by David Lynn. Permission to reproduce this page granted only for use in the buyer's own youth group. www.YouthSpecialties.com

63

WHO'S NUMBER ONE? [putting Christ first]

THIS WEEK

Young Christian teenagers, if they haven't already done so, are about to come to a fork in the spiritual road. When they were younger they attended church, prayed, and memorized Bible verses because that was what they were supposed to do. But now they have a choice. What importance will Christianity take during their adolescence? Use this TalkSheet as an opportunity to talk about the role of Christianity in the lives of your young people.

OPENER

On a white board or poster board, make a list of what your kids think are important. What would an average person consider to be important? Ideas may include food, family, money, health, and friends. Write all these suggestions down. Where does Christ fit into this list? How long did it take your kids before they mentioned Jesus or God? Now ask the group what a non-Christian would consider to be the most important? A celebrity? A government leader? How about a Christian? Point out that people have different priorities and things that are most important to them, based on their beliefs. Where do your kids' beliefs stand? Is Christ first on their list?

THE DISCUSSION, BY NUMBERS

1. How did your kids respond to these statements? What about religions like Islam, the Church of Latter-day Saints (Mormons), Jews, and Jehovah's Witnesses? Can sports, music, video games, or skateboarding be idols? What would God say about having other gods?

2. Make a master list and poll the group (anonymously, if you want). You may be pushed to add an in-between column, "That's Sort of Me." Where do your kids fall in their beliefs? How important are their Christian beliefs to them?

3. How important are their Christian beliefs? You could have the group members rank their involvement in key categories like sports, church stuff, school, and hanging with friends, as one way to measure their commitment. How can your kids make room for God in their lives?

4. Take a vote to see where the majority of your group members rank the commitment level of the people in the verses. Talk about any disagreements and then ask your group what they learned about commitment to their Christian lives.

THE CLOSE

You may want to use the following questions to wrap up the session—How committed do you want to be to your Christian faith? What kind of relationship do you want to have with Jesus Christ? How many things are more important than God?

When God gave the Ten Commandments, he knew that there would be many things that would compete for our attention. This probably explains why the first commandment was first (Exodus 20:3)! Ask your kids this question—what crowds out God in their lives? Whatever it is, that is their god. They are committed to something! Ask the students how much of their commitment is directed toward their Christian faith. How can they get closer to God?

You may want to close with time for prayer, giving your group time with God in silent prayer.

MORE

● How important are their Christian beliefs to your group members? Would they like to set goals for themselves—to get closer to God? To put him first? To spend more time with him and less time in front of the TV? It's important for everyone to have spiritual goals. Encourage each group member to write a letter to themselves—stating their spiritual goals and how they want to grow as closer to God. Give them envelopes, which they will address to themselves and seal. Mail the letters to them anywhere from six months to a year.

● You may want to have your group create a short survey about the importance of one's Christianity. Have your kids e-mail or send this survey to adults, other teenagers, peers, or teachers. Ask each group member to survey three people. Then go over the results to the group and tabulate the results. What did your group observe or learn about commitment to the Christian faith? Did commitment vary among age groups or not?

ECO-CHRISTIANS

1. Which of the following do you (or your family) do?
   - ❏ Recycle newspapers.
   - ❏ Recycle paper and cardboard.
   - ❏ Walk or ride bikes everywhere you can.
   - ❏ Recycle soda cans and bottles.
   - ❏ Throw away pretty much everything.
   - ❏ Use a water-saving appliance in the shower.
   - ❏ Recycle plastic bottles and containers.
   - ❏ Get the car checked for smog and emissions.
   - ❏ Reuse plastic cups and silverware.
   - ❏ Carpool with others to save gas.
   - ❏ Buy paper cups instead of Styrofoam.
   - ❏ Use a garbage disposal in your kitchen.

2. Finish this statement.
   Most students at my school—
   - ❏ Don't care about environmental problems
   - ❏ Care about environmental problems but don't do much about them
   - ❏ Care about environmental problems and do something about them
   - ❏ Are aware of concerns and try to recycle and reuse

3. Which of these do you think are **true**?
   ___ God cares about the environment.
   ___ The Bible offers some practical solutions for today's environmental problems.
   ___ It doesn't matter what becomes of the planet because it's going to be destroyed anyway.
   ___ There is a real Mother Earth.
   ___ Problems with the environment are a sign it is the last days before Christ's return.
   ___ The environmental abuses of today will be taken care of by the time I'm an adult.

4. What is one thing you could do to be a **better steward** of the world God created?
   What could your church do? Your family? Your school?

5. Check out **Psalm 8** and decide what this says to Christians about the environment.

ECO-CHRISTIANS [the environment]

THIS WEEK

There's a lot of emphasis today on environmental issues. Various New Age-influenced movements have used these environmental issues to "evangelize" many. But most young people in the church have little idea about a Christian view of ecology. Those who love God should care for God's world, too! Take this opportunity to talk about a Christian perspective of the environment.

OPENER

Write the following environmental issues on the whiteboard or poster board and ask volunteers to define the problem for each.

Species extinction	Littering
Natural resources depletion	Water pollution
Garbage overload	Hazardous waste
Global warming	Ozone depletion
Acid rain	Air pollution
Greenhouse effect	Rain forest destruction

Do your kids know what these problems are? What are the three most important issues today? What are the most threatening ones for our world?

Or you could test the responsibility of your group. Before the meeting litter your meeting area with some crumpled papers, empty soda cans, some dry cups, and some other (safe) garbage. As your kids walk in check to see if they pick it up or not. Use this litter as an illustration for the TalkSheet—did your kids feel like they should've picked it up? Why or why not?

THE DISCUSSION, BY NUMBERS

1. Which of these do your kids or their families do? Take a poll from the whole group to see which ones are done the most. Why are some reuse/recycling activities easier than others? What difference does each one make?

2. How about other kids in the same peer group? How do other kids in their schools deal with environmental issues? Why do they care or not care? What do schools do to emphasize recycling or reusing?

3. How did your kids answer these? This will let you tie Christianity in with the environment. God does care about the environment—he made it! And he wants your kids to take care of it, too.

4. What can your kids do to be stewards of the earth? What about the church? Schools? Brainstorm a list of ideas and have them decide what to do with this list—could they get things going in the church or school? Could your group start a recycling program? What else could they do?

5. God has given Christians an awesome responsibility to take care of his creation. How does your group think God feels about the kind of job Christians have been doing taking care of his creation?

THE CLOSE

The Bible teaches that people are created in God's image (Genesis 1:26). People are uniquely divided from the animal, plant, and mineral world. Yet, people are united with that world because all of it was created by God and all of it has value (Leviticus 25:23; 1 Chronicles 29:14-16; Psalm 50:10, 11; and Haggai 2:8).

This Christian view of creation gives creation its purpose. God created animals, plants, oceans, and mountains—and they are worth respecting. People are responsible for creation because God created man above everything else. Christians have a responsibility to be good stewards of the earth. But sin has affected creation—people have exploited and abused the earth. But the Bible teaches that the whole of creation awaits God's redemption (Romans 8:18-25). God will fix all of creation when he returns. In the meantime, he's put people—Christians included—in charge of taking care of the world.

MORE

● To tie the lesson in with your group, you may want to have some of your group members take turns recycling the trash, soda cans and bottles, and paper cups accumulated at youth group events. Some states give refunds for soda cans and bottles. You may want to encourage your congregation to bring their recyclable materials to church for the youth group to recycle and use as a fundraiser for your group.

● For more information on the environment, current problems, and solutions, check out OECD Environment (www.oecd.org/env), Friends of the Earth (www.foe.org), Greenpeace (www.greenpeace.org), or Resources for the Future (www.rff.org). If you don't have time to check these out, encourage your kids to! See if they can find some information to share with the group about the environment to share with the group.

FAMILY MATTERS

1. Describe a time you felt really close to your family.

2. On the line below, put an X where you see yourself with your family.

Extremely close to my family　　　　　　　　Way far from close to my family.

3. What is your family like? By each statement write a **T (that's my family)** or **N (that's not my family)**. My family—

___ is as good as it will ever be
___ isn't like any other family I know
___ makes sacrifices for each other
___ fights a lot and doesn't get along
___ cooperates with each other
___ goes to church together
___ isn't any fun at all

___ doesn't spend any time together
___ is abusive and destructive to each other
___ talks about problems and finds solutions
___ is like most other families
___ members are able to talk with each other
___ is hard to be around.
___ has fun together
___ spends the right amount of time together

4. Do you like being a member of your family? Why or why not?

5. Check out these verses below—which passage is the most helpful in dealing with your family life? Why?

Psalm 42:11　　　　Matthew 18:21, 22　　　Ephesians 4:2
Psalm 68:5　　　　 Romans 12:12　　　　　1 John 3:1-3
Proverbs 11:29　　 Galatians 5:22, 23　　　1 John 4:10-12

FAMILY MATTERS [f a m i l y   l i f e]

THIS WEEK

The structure of the family has undergone enormous changes in recent years. Today there are different types of families within society—traditional families, divorced families, single-parent families, or foster families. This TalkSheet will let you talk with your kids about their families and the role of family in their lives.

Pay close attention to your group during this discussion. Don't assume that all your kids live in a traditional two-parent home! Be extra sensitive to those kids who may be feeling the hurt and confusion of divorce and family separation.

OPENER

You can do this intro a few different ways. First, create some artificial families in your group—either simply split your group up into smaller groups, or actually link the family together using yarn to loosely tie together four or five group members at the wrists. Include both girls and boys in each family—you'll need at least two feet of yarn per person (you can assign a mom, dad, and siblings, if you want). Once these family ties are fastened, you can do different activities with the "family." Here are a few suggestions—

- Have the group create an ice cream sundae to eat with each other.
- Give each group a candy bar to open and divide among themselves.
- Plan a family vacation together and decide where they'll go and what to do.
- The M&M relay. Each family member has to run, pick up a certain color M&M with their toes—and then eat it!
- The bandana relay. There's a pile of bandanas on one side of the room. The family members must put a bandana on—but can't put it on themselves. They have to help each other tie one on their heads. The first group with bandanas on wins.

Afterward, cut the yarn and talk about how your kids felt being tied together. Did they feel limited in what they could do? What was hard about being tied together? How is this an analogy of their families (even though they aren't literally tied together!)?

THE DISCUSSION, BY NUMBERS

1. You'll want to make sure that your kids feel comfortable sharing these experiences. Some won't feel comfortable sharing unless they are reasonably sure their peers won't put them down. Begin by sharing one of your own junior high school experiences of closeness with your family.

2. You may want to ask for a general response to this one—for example, ask how many of your kids ranked themselves more to the right than to the left. Get a feel for the relationships of your group members to their families. Are your kids satisfied with their current family relationship? Why or why not?

3. As some of them talk about their families, remind the group of your confidentiality rule. You may want to talk about this anonymously, if your kids aren't open to sharing. Then brainstorm ways group members can build up their families.

4. What does it takes to be a proud member of a family? If your kids don't want to share their answers, that's okay. Let the group members know that you will be available to talk with them privately about their personal concerns related to family life.

5. Read each of these passages with your group. Were these helpful in dealing with their family lives? Why or why not? What does God have to say about families?

THE CLOSE

Affirm the need for family, but be sensitive to those kids in your group with broken families. Point out that every family is different, because each person is different. But no matter what your kids' situations are, you can play a vital role in supporting family life by what you say. You may want to form a circle and pray for each other's families. And encourage any of them who may want to talk about their families with you to do so. Some of your kids might need some individual encouragement and insight. Encourage them to find an adult who they are comfortable with to talk to.

MORE

- You may want to challenge your kids to ask questions of some of their family members. They may find out stuff about their family that they never know before! Below are some questions to use as a guide. Questions could include: Who were you named after? Did you have a nickname? What games did you play growing up?
- You may want to talk about family situations that aren't healthy. Some of your kids may be in—or have friends who are in—unhealthy, abusive family situations. For more information, check out the National Exchange Club Foundation (www.preventchildabuse.com) or the American Humane Association (www.americanhumane.org), Rape, Abuse, and Incest National Network (www.rainn.org), The Family Violence Prevention Fund (www.fvpf.org), or Christians In Recovery (www.christians-in-recovery.com).

TOP OF THE LIST

1. What is the **absolute, number one, biggest, most important priority** in your life?

2. Check the **five most important** things in your life right now.
   - ❑ Getting good grades
   - ❑ Making money
   - ❑ Being cool
   - ❑ Finding out how to get close to God
   - ❑ Watching your favorite TV shows
   - ❑ Being good at a sport
   - ❑ Surfing the Internet
   - ❑ Getting high
   - ❑ Wearing the right clothes
   - ❑ Spending time with your family
   - ❑ Having the right friends
   - ❑ Participating in church activities
   - ❑ Being on a sports team at school
   - ❑ Dealing with your family situation
   - ❑ Talking to people about Jesus Christ
   - ❑ Having fun
   - ❑ Volunteering to help others
   - ❑ Playing video games
   - ❑ Having a boyfriend or girlfriend
   - ❑ Helping out a friend who is suffering

3. Which of these statements you think are **untrue**?
   - ❑ Kids my age don't need to worry about priorities.
   - ❑ The Bible doesn't say anything about priorities.
   - ❑ If people don't have priorities, they'll have unhappy lives
   - ❑ Adults do a better job at ordering their priorities than teenagers.
   - ❑ Priorities are important for everyone, regardless of age
   - ❑ Church doesn't have to be a priority for someone to live the Christian life.

4. Draw a line connecting these Bible references with the correct summarized statements below.

a. Proverbs 3:6	1. Seek God's priorities and everything else will fall into place.
b. Matthew 7:21	2. Obeying Christ's teachings shows our love for him.
c. Luke 9:23	3. Recognize God in your priorities and he will make you successful.
d. Luke 12:31	4. Not everyone who says God is number one truly believes in their heart that God is number one.
e. John 14:23	5. Willingness to do what Christ wants demonstrates our desire to make God number one.
f. Romans 12:2	6. Caring about others should be a top priority for God's people.
g. 1 Peter 4:8	7. God wants us to conform to his will and his desires rather than being like the world.

TOP OF THE LIST [p r i o r i t i e s]

THIS WEEK

In a culture that pulls kids in all directions, it's sometimes difficult for them to know what's the most important thing in their lives. This TalkSheet takes an honest look at the priorities of young people and will help your students see why God needs to be in the center of their lives and priorities.

OPENER

To start, give you kids a list of different tasks that they may have to do on a given day. You can either hand this list out to individual groups or write the list on a whiteboard or poster board. A few examples can include things like—

* Going to bed on time (getting enough sleep)
* Taking a shower or bath
* Eating three meals a day
* Helping your mom or dad out around the house
* Doing your homework
* Going to basketball (or whatever sport) practice
* Spending some time with God
* Getting up on time in the morning
* Hanging with your friends
* Exercising to keep yourself healthy
* Checking your e-mail or surfing the Internet
* Going shopping for new clothes or other stuff

Go ahead and add whatever other things you'd like to add. Now ask your kids to prioritize this list from 1-12 (12 being the most important thing on this list). If you split your group into smaller groups, ask each group to share its prioritized list. Then, come to a consensus with the whole group. How did your kids decide which was most important? Least important? How might these priorities change as they get older? What priorities may be added in the future? Use this activity as a springboard for discussion on priorities.

THE DISCUSSION, BY NUMBERS

1. Many kids will tell you what you want to hear. Challenge the students to look at what they really like to spend their time doing.

2. This question expands on the introduction. Have the group work together to prioritize the five most important things. Then ask the young people to identify the five most important things for kids who aren't Christians. Compare and contrast these two lists.

3. As you have the young people reveal their answers to these statements, ask them to reflect on the previous activity of comparing their answers with those of kids who aren't Christians.

4. Invite the group to ask questions about the Bible's perspective on priorities. Have individuals share what they learned from the passages. Get practical with ways kids can make God number one in their lives—service to God through service to others, learning more about God, and so on.

THE CLOSE

Point out to your group that priorities can be easy to set but hard to live out. But what's most important is what's on their hearts—what really matters to them and what God puts on their hearts. Matthew 6:21 says "For where your priorities are, there your heart will be also" (author's paraphrase). As your kids live their daily priorities out, these priorities will become etched on their hearts. And God will work in their hearts to show them what's really important.

Challenge your kids to examine their priorities. What would honor and serve God the most? How can your kids being to re-prioritize their lives? How can being close to God make it easier to figure out their priorities? Close with a time of prayer, asking God to show you and your kids his priorities for them.

MORE

* To take this further, you may want to have the group members keep a priority log that contains all of the things they did during the week. Then have them bring their logs back to the group and talk about how well they were able to live out their priorities. How did they handle these priorities? How could they have done better? How may their priorities differ from their parents? Teachers? Pastor? Employer?

* What does society say about priorities? You may want to have your kids pay attention to the media this week—particularly TV advertisements, commercials, and magazine ads. What do these ads say about prioritizing and getting what you want? What do TV shows say about what's most important? Take some time to talk about these with your group and have them bring in some examples. Then ask them this question—how does the media influence our priorities? And what can they do to keep their priorities straight when the media says different things?

MASQUERADE

1. What does the word **hypocrisy** mean to you?

2. What do you think? The main reason why **Christian** young people act like hypocrites is because—
   - ❑ They cave in to peer pressure
   - ❑ That's the way teenagers are
   - ❑ They are forced to be hypocrites by their parents or guardians
   - ❑ They know what they're doing is wrong but they do it anyway
   - ❑ They don't know any better
   - ❑ They're just being rebellious
   - ❑ Other—

3. Do you think each of these statements is **T (true)** or **F (false)**?
   ___ If you're in junior high or middle school, you have to be a hypocrite to survive.
   ___ Some people are bigger hypocrites than others.
   ___ Being a hypocrite is the same thing, no matter how big of one you are.
   ___ People are hypocrites because they worry about what others think of them.
   ___ Christians are less hypocritical than other people.

4. How often do you live what you believe?
   - ❑ Every day
   - ❑ Most every day
   - ❑ Some days
   - ❑ Sundays
   - ❑ No days

5. Why is it easier to see hypocrisy in someone else than it is to see it in yourself?

6. Look up **Matthew 7:3-5** and write how you think Christ's words apply specifically to you.

71

MASQUERADE [p e r s o n a l   h y p o c r i s y]

THIS WEEK

Do your kids know what it means to practice what they preach? Or to live by what they believe? This TalkSheet will give you an opportunity to talk about hypocrisy with your kids. You'll need to be sensitive to the spiritual condition of the individuals in your group—some may be more into Christianity than others. Keep an open and honest discussion with your kids. And be careful not to be too judgmental or heavy handed—your goal isn't to drive the kids into hypocrisy, but closer to the Lord.

OPENER

Do your kids know what a masquerade is? A masquerade is a costume dance, where people dress up with full costumes and masks. Most often people don't know who they are dancing with due to the masks! You may want to introduce this topic about being two-faced by bringing in several masks to the group. There are usually many around during Halloween time, or you can get some from any costume shop. Ask some kids to come forward and try on the masks. Then ask them why people like the masquerade dances and dressing up on Halloween. Why do bank robbers and other criminals cover their faces with ski masks? People want to get away with things they normally wouldn't do. They want to feel safe by hiding their faces. Hypocrisy is exactly like wearing a mask—people pretend to be someone that they're not, and they think they're getting away with something. What other masks do junior highers or middle schoolers put on? How do kids their age keep others from seeing who they really are?

THE DISCUSSION, BY NUMBERS

1. With your group, come up with a definition of hypocrisy. Write it in a place where everyone can see it so you can refer to it later in the discussion.

2. Poll the group to find out the two or three biggest reasons Christian young people act like hypocrites. Why does this happen? Does being a hypocrite help the situation or hurt it?

3. Point out that hypocrisy is a survival skill. How much of a reality is this for the members of your group? What are other alternatives to hypocrisy for surviving in junior high or middle school? How do Christians compare to other people? How is it for your kids to be Christians in their own schools?

4. This question forces your kids to examine how consistently they practice what they preach. If you don't want to ask for individual answers, ask your kids how often Christian kids their age practice what they preach? How about non-Christian kids? Their teachers? Parents? Pastors?

5. Let different group members share their opinions. How can your kids better identify their own hypocrisy rather than judging others? What does God say about judging others (Luke 6:37)?

6. How do these verses apply to your kids? If you choose not to ask for volunteers, you may want to give an example from your own life. If your group feels safe with each other, encourage them to share their answers with each other.

THE CLOSE

One way to look at hypocrisy is to view it as the opposite of repentance. Instead of realizing a sin and confessing it, a hypocrite pretends to ignore the problem. The hypocrite goes through the Christian motions for the purpose of fooling others or perhaps himself or herself. Young people need to realize that everyone is hypocritical to some extent. People are hypocrites every time they judge one another (Matthew 7:1) and are hypocrites every time they talk about their sin in the past tense (1 John 1:8). The Bible warns against being deceived by sin—, which causes hypocrisy (Jeremiah 17:9; Romans 7:11; and 1 Corinthians 3:18).

What can your kids do to be less hypocritical? How can a stronger relationship with God help them and others be less hypocritical? What can your kids do today to get right with God and others? Close with a time of prayer with your group.

MORE

● Where have your kids seen hypocrisy in society in the past few months or year? Has there been a celebrity or other famous person that has been hypocritical—and gotten caught? Be careful not to put judgment on these people—instead, ask your group what ramifications may come with being hypocritical. Do celebrities and other famous people have more responsibility than others? Why or why not? How does fame or popularity affect how people act? How about Christians who are in these situations? Do they have a greater responsibility?

● How does hypocrisy compare to lying? What do your kids think is worse—having a friend lie to them or act hypocritical toward them? You may want to role-play a situation like this or ask your kids to describe a situation of hypocrisy to act out. Which do they think is worse—being two-faced or flat-out lying?

TOO MUCH TOO SOON

1. Circle or **three** words below that describe how you feel about **sex**.

Scared	Sinful	Strange
Pure	Confused	Hurtful
Pleasure	Unbelievable	Perverse
Painful	Weird	Awesome
Moral	Excited	Sick
Disgusted	Sanctified	

2. What would most people at your school say about the following statements?

a. It isn't a good thing to be a virgin in high school.
- ❑ Most people at my school would say this is true.
- ❑ Most people at my school would say this isn't true.

b. It's more acceptable for a guy to have sex than for a girl to have sex.
- ❑ Most people at my school would say this is true.
- ❑ Most people at my school would say this isn't true.

c. Teenagers can't be stopped from having sex.
- ❑ Most people at my school would say this is true.
- ❑ Most people at my school would say this isn't true.

d. Our school teaches us what we need to know about sex.
- ❑ Most people at my school would say this is true.
- ❑ Most people at my school would say this isn't true.

3. What do you think? Is each item below either **M (a myth/false info)** about sex or **R (a reality)** of having sex?

___ You might get a sexually transmitted disease.
___ Your parents might find out.
___ Being a player gives you a good reputation.
___ The girl might get pregnant.
___ Sexual intimacy equals love.
___ Sex can be a scary experience.
___ You might get hurt emotionally.
___ God wants you to wait until you're married.
___ Teenagers are too young to be parents.
___ Sex is okay if you love the person, even though you aren't married.
___ Sex isn't good for you.
___ Sex before marriage can hurt a relationship.

4. Check out each of these verses—what do they say about sex?

Proverbs 5:18, 19	1 Corinthians 6:18-20
Romans 7:4-6	1 Thessalonians 4:3-8

TOO MUCH TOO SOON [premarital sex]

THIS WEEK

Teenagers today are bombarded with the message that premarital sex is acceptable. Because the media, peers, and teachers tell them that it's okay, they need to hear the other side of the story in a positive, non-judgmental way. This TalkSheet discusses sexuality in a Christian context. Be sensitive to your group members during this discussion. Some of your group member may be—or know someone who is—sexually active. Your goal is to let them know God's views of sex and not lay a guilt trip on your kids.

OPENER

Society has warped the meaning of sex in a number of ways. TV shows, movies, Internet pornographic sites, and other media have given the wrong messages about sex. Ask the group to list where sex is shown, talked about, referred to, and sung about, in the media. What words has your group heard or learned that describe sex? Be careful—you may get some offensive slang words. Why have people used these words to describe sex? If sex was created by God—a beautiful thing, for pleasure—why has society desecrated it? How do they think society has twisted the meaning of sex? Why or why not?

THE DISCUSSION, BY NUMBERS

1. Without putting pressure on kids to give direct answers, obtain a group consensus about how kids feel about sex. What do they think kids their age in general think about sex? Be sensitive to the variety of perspectives suggested. Some of the kids in your group may already have had negative experiences, such as sexual abuse or premarital sex. Point out that sex can be viewed in both positive and negative ways depending upon attitudes and behaviors.

2. This question is a gauge for the sexual attitudes of your group. These attitudes will shape their present and future sexual behaviors. After letting the group members share their opinions of their peers at school, encourage them in sharing their own views. Begin sharing what God might have to say about virginity, the double standard, and controlling sexual urges.

3. What myths or realities do your kids—or teenagers in general—believe about sex? Take some time to talk about these statements with your kids and answer any questions they may have.

4. Make a list of the differences between what society says about sex and what God says. Ask the group to decide which standard makes the most sense and why.

THE CLOSE

For sexual lives to be the best, Christians need to follow God's sexual directions given to us in the Bible. Make it very clear that God forgives any sin—even sexual sins—and he is listening to anyone who comes to him. You may wish to read a few verses about God's forgiveness and compassion—Isaiah 1:18 or 1 John 1:9. Encourage your kids to get right with God and to ask them for his self-control (a fruit of the Holy Spirit) and wisdom. God wants the best for them, which is why he gave them boundaries to stick with!

Some of your kids have dealt with rape, sexual abuse, or abortion. Communicate with your kids that under no circumstances should anyone sexually abuse or rape another person. Both are crimes, punished by years in prison (or worse). If your kids are victims of inappropriate comments, touches, or sexual aggression—or suspect others are—they must get help immediately from a school counselor, parent, pastor, or you. For more information, visit the Rape, Abuse, and Incest National Network (www.rainn.org) or National Coalition Against Sexual Assault (http://ncasa.org).

You may want to close by reading 1 Thessalonians 4:1-8 and a time of prayer for your kids to bring their concerns, fears, and hurts to God.

MORE

- You may want to talk with your kids about what they can do to help a friend who is caught in a sexual situation—facing an abuse family member, contemplating abortion, or recovering from a rape. How would they handle these situations? Where would they go? What would be the best thing for them to do—for their friend and themselves?
- If you haven't done this in the lesson Sexual Stuff, you may want to talk about abstinence with your group. If you feel your group is interested, end with a challenge to commit to abstinence. How can your kids promote abstinence among themselves? For information, check out Aim for Success (www.aim-for-success.org), True Love Waits (www.truelovewaits.com), or the Youth Specialties Web page (www.YouthSpecialties.com) for links to information and resources.

SATAN & CO.

1. Circle three of the words you think of when you hear or read the word **Satan**.

Spooky	Enemy	Unreal
Harmless	Ugly	Deceptive
Liar	Rebellious	Demons
Horns	Terrifying	Halloween
Black	Hell	Ungodly
Tricky	Occult	Harmless
Evil	Pitchfork	Powerful

2. Which of the following things do you think are satanic?

❑ Horoscopes
❑ Ouija board playing
❑ Halloween
❑ Violent music
❑ Channeling
❑ Witchcraft
❑ Spirit guides
❑ Levitation games

❑ Novels with an occult theme
❑ Fortune-telling
❑ Fantasy role-playing games
❑ Horror movies
❑ Drug use
❑ Séances
❑ Crystals
❑ Other—

3. Check the statement that you think is most **true**.
   Our church believes that—
   ❑ Satan doesn't exist.
   ❑ Satan exists but isn't a threat to Christians.
   ❑ Christians must take Satan and his demonic influence more seriously.
   ❑ God will one day crush Satan because Jesus conquered sin and death.
   ❑ Satan is very powerful and is out to destroy Christians.
   ❑ Satan can't get near you if you are God's child.

4. You get home two hours before your parents do and usually spent time doing homework, playing computer games, watching TV, surfing the Internet, or just hanging out. Today your friend shows up at your house with an Ouija board.
   What should you do?
   What are the dangers of playing games like this—Ouija board and similar Internet games?
   Why do some kids think these games are harmless?
   What could this situation say about your friend?

5. Check out the following Bible verses and write what each one says about standing against Satan.
   Ephesians 6:10-18
   James 4:7
   1 Peter 5:8, 9

SATAN & CO. [satanism]

THIS WEEK

Too many times talking about the satanic will spark curiosity in kids and the next thing you know, they're logging onto every satanic Web site on the Internet for more information. This discussion shouldn't focus on the gory details of satanic rituals and worship, but should address the realities of satanic involvement by today's teenagers—and the dangers of getting involved.

OPENER

You may want to ask your group members to name all of the movies or TV shows that contain demonic or satanic themes. You may want to make a list of these for all to see (you may be able to learn a thing or two!). Point out the growing trend in our culture toward the satanic. Is this healthy or unhealthy? How should Christians react to this? Why do your kids think there is such an interest in the demonic?

Or read to your group the story of Christ and Satan in the desert (Matthew 4:1-11). What does this story say about Satan and his power? How did he try to trick Jesus? If he tries to trick Jesus, can he trick us today?

THE DISCUSSION, BY NUMBERS

1. What words did your kids choose and why? Make a master list of all the words. Where do your kids get these ideas? How much does the media influence their ideas? What about the church?

2. You'll get a variety of responses here. Explain to the group that Satan works through each of the items listed. Satan is called the Father of Lies—he will use anything he can to deceive people.

3. Take some time to explain what your church believes. You may want to have your senior pastor on hand to help answer questions from your kids.

4. How many of your kids have been tempted to dabble in satanic things like Ouija boards, tarot cards, or spiritualistic Internet games? Do they have friends who are into these things? With your group, brainstorm ways they can resist the devil. And be sure to stress the importance of steering clear of these games—even those that seem harmless. Satan can use those lead-ins to get them hooked into wanting to know more.

5. What do these verses say about Christianity and Satan? You may want to divide the group into small groups and have each group take a different passage of Scripture. Allow enough time for them to reach a consensus on what they think the passage says about what a Christian's response to the Satan should be.

THE CLOSE

Point out that one of Satan's strategies is to convince people that he doesn't exist. The other strategy is to convince people he is real and can provide them with power. That's appealing to some young people—especially those who feel powerless and who don't know the truth. Only the one true God has the power for living, fills people with joy and peace, and loves them unconditionally.

Emphasize the reality of Satan and the evil work he and his demons are carrying out in today's world. This can be effectively and quickly done by pointing out some of the names the Bible has given Satan—Tempter (Matthew 4:3), Liar (John 8:44), Enemy (1 Peter 5:8), Evil One (1 John 5:19), and Accuser (Revelation 12:10). Also emphasize that Christ came to destroy the work of the Devil (1 John 3:8), and that Christ—who dwells in every Christian through the Holy Spirit—is greater than Satan (1 John 4:4).

What's the most powerful tool for protection from Satan? Prayer. It's the Christian warrior's tool against Satan. Encourage your kids to pray for God's protection and to pray for the leaders in the church, like the pastors, elders, and other leaders. Close with a time of prayer, asking for God to shield, protect, and lead your group and those that they love.

MORE

- Some of your kids may have dabbled in satanism or have friends who have. Take some more time to talk about the dangers of getting involved in this—even for innocent fun. What can your kids do if they or others are hooked on satanism? What can you do to pull them back? For more information, check out Cult Awareness & Information Center (www.caic.org.au), Apologetics Research Resources on Religious Cults, Sects, Movements, Doctrines, Etc. (www.gospelcom.net/apologeticsindex), or www.YouthSpecialties.com for more links.

- How did other biblical characters deal with Satan? Have your group find more references to Satan in the Bible and talk about these with your group. Are there other stories where he is directly involved? For example, how did Satan trick Eve in the Garden of Eden? What does this story say about Satan? What else does the Bible reveal about Satan? Where do your kids think Satan came from? Do they know the story of how he got kicked out of Heaven?

MISSION IMPOSSIBLE?

1. What one word best describes the **opposite sex**?

2. Complete the following sentences.

   Most girls think guys are—

   Most guys think girls are—

3. What do you think—**T (true)** or **F (false)**?
   ___ Girls and guys can be best friends.
   ___ Christians should only date other Christians.
   ___ It's okay for a girl to ask a boy to go out.
   ___ Guys are more committed to Christ than girls.
   ___ Junior high or middle school is too early for kids to be dating.
   ___ Girls and guys can't communicate well.
   ___ Most junior high or middle school students get into opposite-sex relationships because everyone else is.
   ___ If your parents don't approve of the person you're seeing, you should stop seeing them.
   ___ All guys think about is getting physical and having sex.
   ___ A young person my age can't be in love.
   ___ Girls want opposite-sex relationships more than guys.

4. What do you think? Are these situations **harmless** or **risky**? Why?
   You're at a party and people start playing games involving kissing.

   You're close friends with a member of the opposite sex and you start liking that person.

   You're asked out by a member of the opposite sex.

   You're home alone after school when a close friend of the opposite sex stops by to hang out.

5. If you could ask all members of the opposite sex **one question**, what would it be?

6. Match the verses with the statements on the right.

   a. Romans 15:7   1. Love each other.
   b. Galatians 5:13   2. Pray for each other.
   c. Ephesians 6:18   3. Serve each other.
   d. 1 Thessalonians 5:11 4. Accept each other.
   e. 1 Peter 1:22   5. Encourage each other.

From *More Junior High-Middle School TalkSheets—Updated!* by David Lynn. Permission to reproduce this page granted only for use in the buyer's own youth group. www.YouthSpecialties.com

77

MISSION IMPOSSIBLE? [relating to the opposite sex]

THIS WEEK

Junior highers and middle schoolers often have many questions and concerns about the opposite sex that go unanswered. As kids get older, they become closer friends with the opposite sex. This TalkSheet will help deal with the confusion about relationships and communication with the opposite sex—and answer to their questions and look at opposite sex relationships from a Christian perspective. See More Than Friends (page 15), and Sexual Stuff (page 13).

OPENER

For this intro, you may want to illustrate the differences in thinking among girls and guys. To start, call two volunteers—a guy and a girl—to the front of the group. Let the girl leave the room and read a situation to the guy in front of the group and give him a chance to react to the situation. Ask the group to notice how the guy answered or reacted to the situation. Now let the girl in and read her the same situation. How did she react? Ask the group the differences they noticed between how each answered. What does this say about girl versus guy communication? Is it fair to assume that all guys (or all girls) think and communicate the same way? Why or why not?

Need a few situations to get started? How about these—

- You've just been cut from the team and your best friends made it. How do you react?
- You've just gotten a low (almost failing) grade on the hardest exam you've ever taken. How are you feeling?
- You just found out that there is a girl (or guy) that likes you. What will you do about it?
- Your sister or brother hits you hard—and I mean hard. What are you going to do?
- Your mom and dad are splitting up—for good. What will you tell your friends?
- A kid in the hallway cusses at you. What are you going to do about it?

THE DISCUSSION, BY NUMBERS

1. Make a master list of the words that your kids chose and why. Keep the list of questions running throughout the discussion and have the group answer them at the end of the session.

2. How did your kids complete these statements? Give both sexes their chance to defend their position.

3. This activity stresses the importance of thinking through relationships. Some kids this age rush into romantic relationships before they are ready. Emphasize the importance of maintaining strong ties to Christian friends of both sexes—and to keep a close relationship with God.

4. As you move through each situation, ask your kids to give a Christian perspective on each. How may Christians handle the situations differently than non-Christians?

5. What questions do your kids have? Keep a list of these questions and take some time to answer them. You may want to have your adult leaders help you answer these, as well as other kids in your group.

6. Read these passages and ask how the verses relate to a Christian's relationship with the opposite sex. What does God say about friendships and romantic relationships to the opposite sex?

THE CLOSE

You may want to illustrate the friendship between Jesus and Mary Magdalene (Luke 8:2 and John 20), and Mary and Martha (Luke 10:38-42). Jesus had close relationships with women in the Bible—yet was never romantically involved with them. How can your kids reflect the love of Jesus in their relationships with the opposite sex?

Also, point out that there's nothing wrong with some kids who aren't interested yet in the opposite sex—that's okay. Don't allow anyone to make fun of them or accuse them of being homosexual. Close with a time of prayer with your group and give your kids time to pray for their friends and relationships.

MORE

- You may want to ask a panel of people—including parents, high schoolers, college students, and some grandparents—for a Q&A session with your group. Encourage your kids to ask questions about how to relate to the opposite sex. How do relationships and friendships change in high school and in college? How can girls and guys get to be better friends? How are friendships and dating situations different?
- What does the media say about girl and guy relationships? How often do friends in movies or TV shows land up in dating relationships? You may want to ask your kids what TV shows or movies they've seen where friendships turn into romantic relationships. What happened? Was the outcome good or bad?

THIEF IN THE NIGHT

1. When you think about the **return of Christ**, how do you feel? (Circle one)

   Excited   Cheated
   Depressed   At peace
   Sad   Worried
   Relieved   Frustrated
   Scared   Happy
   Uncertain   Motivated
   Indifferent   Other—

2. If someone asked you what the Bible says about Christ's return, what would you tell them?

3. How would you respond to these statements—
   S (sometimes), O (often), or **N (never)**?
   ___ I worry about the future.
   ___ I wonder when Christ will return.
   ___ I would like to learn more about Christ's second coming.
   ___ I wonder what it will be like when Christ comes back.
   ___ I have a good relationship with the living Christ today.
   ___ I wonder what heaven and hell are like.
   ___ I'm prepared for the return of Jesus Christ.

4. If you knew for sure that Christ would return in a month, how would you live your life differently during the next 30 days?

5. Write down **three questions** you have about Christ's return.

6. Check out the verses below and then connect each one with the appropriate statement.
   a. Joel 2:31, 32   1. Christ is coming soon.
   b. Matthew 24:42   2. Live holy and godly lives.
   c. Titus 2:13   3. Call on the name of the Lord.
   d. 2 Peter 3:11   4. Keep watch.
   e. Revelation 3:11   5. Wait for the blessed hope.

From *More Junior High-Middle School TalkSheets—Updated!* by David Lynn. Permission to reproduce this page granted only for use in the buyer's own youth group. www.YouthSpecialties.com

79

THIEF IN THE NIGHT [Christ's return]

THIS WEEK

Many junior high or middle schoolers are fascinated with the book of Revelation and the end of the world. They want to know about the future and what it holds for them. What do your kids think about Christ's return? This TalkSheet will let you openly talk about the return of Christ with your group.

OPENER

You may want to start by splitting your group up into smaller groups and giving each group a different set of Bible verses to read (you can combine these if you don't have enough groups for all the verses)—
- Luke 12:40, Luke 17:23-24
- Matthew 24:40-50
- Revelation 6:12-17
- 1 Thessalonians 5:1-3
- Isaiah 13:6-12
- Zephaniah 1:14-18
- Matthew 25:1-13
- Matthew 25:14-30
- Matthew 25:31-46
- 1 Corinthians 15:51-57
- 1 Thessalonians 4:15-18
- Revelation 21:1-8
- Revelation 20:11-15
- Isaiah 34:4, Joel 3:15-16, Zechariah 14:4

All these verses describe the second coming of Christ—some are parables, so you might have to help your kids out! After each group has read their verse, gather as a group and have each group summarize each set of verses. You may want to have some groups read their verses aloud. Make a master list of what the second coming will be like. How do these verses make your kids feel? What do these verses say about the power and authority of Christ? What assurance can Christians have about his return?

THE DISCUSSION, BY NUMBERS

1. How do your kids feel about the second coming of Christ? Be sensitive to your group members' reaction, and never use the second coming or other prophecies as a scare tactic.

2. What do your kids know or think about the return of Christ? How many of the verses or parables from the intro did your kids know? Point out that immediately after Christ went into heaven, he promised to return again (Acts 1:11).

3. Focus on your group's preparation for Christ's return. What sort of relationship do the kids have with the Lord and with others? What do they wonder or have questions about?

4. How would your kids live their lives differently if they knew when Christ would come back? What kind of life does God wants each of us to live in light of his return (Titus 2:11-14)? Why not start to live right today?!

5. Keep track of your kids' questions. You can either answer them now or save them for later— you may want to do some biblical research and or talk with the senior pastor. Better yet, bring him in to answer the questions up front!

6. Ask for some volunteers to read these passages. How did they match them up? How can your kids personalize each of these verses for their lives today?

THE CLOSE

You may have had a lot of questions and discussion items during this TalkSheet. Summarize the different points made during the discussion. What did your kids learn about the return of Christ? How have their feelings or views of Christ changed? Why or why not? Explain that the return of Christ is uncertain, and may be a bit scary. But those who love Jesus don't have anything to worry about—but they've got to be ready for him to come anytime. Finally, close with this challenge for your group: Jesus told us in his own words that no one will know when he will return (Matthew 24:36)—but he will return. Are they ready?

MORE

- You may want to invite the pastor of your church to answer the group's questions regarding Christ's return. Here are some questions to get the discussion going—
  - ⇒ Why is the return of Christ so important?
  - ⇒ What will happen when Christ does return?
  - ⇒ When do you think Christ will return?
  - ⇒ Why didn't Jesus tell us when he was coming back?
  - ⇒ How has the doctrine of the second coming of
  - ⇒ Christ affected your life?
- If you want to talk more about the second coming of Christ, consider taking this TalkSheet further. Spend some time reading some passages from Revelation and talking about them with your group. This is sometimes a hard chapter to grasp the meaning of—if you choose to do this, make sure that your group is interested in learning more. Check out the *Teen Devotional Bible* (Zondervan) for editor's notes and further explanations. Or use a Bible reference guide or handbook, to help your kids understand the passages.

DO CHEATERS PROSPER?

1. How many people at your school do you think cheat?
   - ❏ No one
   - ❏ Less than half
   - ❏ About half
   - ❏ More than half
   - ❏ Everyone

2. What do you think students at your school cheat on the most?
   - ❏ Tests and quizzes
   - ❏ Homework
   - ❏ Book reports
   - ❏ Projects

3. Do you agree with this statement?
   Cheating pays off.

   Why or why not?

4. Is it cheating? Read each of the following statements and decide is each one is
   S (serious cheating), B (barely cheating), or **N (not really cheating).**

   a. _____ Copying off of someone's test paper.

   b. _____ Writing answers on your arm or hand for a test.

   c. _____ Allowing your parent or guardian to do a homework assignment.

   d. _____ Asking someone sitting near you for the answer to a test question.

   e. _____ Copying someone else's book report from last year.

   f. _____ Letting a friend copy answers from your test.

   g. _____ Telling a friend an answer to a test question.

   h. _____ Letting another student help you on a special project.

   i. _____ Letting someone copy an answer from your homework.

   j. _____ Copying an answer from someone else's homework.

   k. _____ Changing an answer for someone when papers are exchanged for grading purposes.

   l. _____ Asking someone to change an answer for you when papers are exchanged for grading purposes.

   m. _____ Taking information straight off the Internet when you're writing a paper.

5. Choose one of the following verses to rewrite in your own words—how does it apply to cheating?
   Leviticus 19:11
   Psalm 101:7
   Matthew 16:26

DO CHEATERS PROSPER? [cheating]

THIS WEEK

Cheating is an easy way out for some middle schoolers and junior highers. As peer pressure intensifies during this time, so does the pressure to cheat in school—and it's become more and more common. Some of your kids—and others their age—lack the experience, skills, and values to say no to cheating. This TalkSheet discusses this critical honesty issue.

OPENER

To start, you may want to make up a short quiz about your church to give to the group. The quiz could ask questions like—

- How many bathrooms are there in our church?
- What was last week's sermon about?
- What translation of the Bible does the pastor use?
- What was the theme of the past summer's camp?
- What is the name of a missionary supported by our church?
- Who is our church secretary?

Pass the quiz out to each member of the group and point out that there will be a prize for the person with the most correct answers. Then ask them to answer the questions by themselves—with no talking. Then leave the room for a minute or two. When you come back in the room, ask them stop working on the quiz and put their pencils down.

Now ask your kids if they thought anyone in the room cheated (they may know exactly who did, but don't let them give names). If people did cheat, how did they cheat? If there was no cheating on the quiz, why? What makes people want to cheat? Evaluate what happened when you left the room and the responses of your group.

THE DISCUSSION, BY NUMBERS

1. Talk about the peer pressure to cheat. The pressure to cheat increases in high school—why might this be true? Often it's true because of the competitive academic pressure with college-bound students, or because of the opposite problem—students who just want to get by.

2. What do kids in schools cheat on most? Why do they cheat on some items more than others? Point out that research indicates that as the chance of getting caught cheating goes up, the rate of cheating goes down. Cheating—including plagiarism (copying or writing something that's not yours)—can lead to serious problems. How often do your kids think others plagiarize? Where from? The Internet? Books? Encyclopedias?

3. Ask the young people what they think of the title of this TalkSheet. Do cheaters prosper? How do they prosper? What will happen to you if you choose not to cheat? What happens if one gets caught cheating?

4. Many young people are confused about what cheating actually is, especially in specific situations. Some of these are active cheating (a, b, d, e, j, k, l) while others are passive cheating (c, f, g, h, i). Once you've debated each statement, talk about passive and active cheating and point out that both are examples of cheating.

5. Ask for volunteers to read their paraphrased passages. Then talk about each of these passages as they relate to cheating.

THE CLOSE

Point out that cheating is stealing—it's taking something that isn't rightfully yours. Students who cheat take something they don't deserve—and often get away with it. But getting away doesn't make it the right way to live.

Cheaters will cheat in any situation—as long as they don't get caught. This loose standard and twisted thinking will get kids into deep trouble—especially in high school and college. And if they can get away with it, they'll keep doing it. Soon everything in their lives becomes dishonest.

God has given each of your kids a mind with the ability to learn and achieve. How do your kids feel when they do well, knowing that they tried hard—even if they fail? How do they cheat themselves when they cheat or plagiarize? How does God feel? Is cheating the best way to honor him?

MORE

- Have your kids do some research on penalties and punishment for cheating and plagiarism. What punishments to their teachers enforce? What about the government? What happens in a high school or university if someone is caught cheating or plagiarizing something that's not theirs? See what your kids can find out—encourage them to ask, call, or e-mail their teachers, local high schools, and colleges.
- What occurrences of cheating happen that aren't just school related? Where do your kids see or experience cheating in the real world? On their sports teams? At their jobs? Where do your kids see cheating shown on TV or in the movies? Have they seen people getting caught cheating? What does society say about cheating? How does this compare with Christianity's view of cheating?

"MY PARENT'S SPLIT UP"

1. List **three** words that you think best describe how most teenagers feel after their parents split up or divorce.

2. Which of the following family situations affects teenagers most negatively?
   - ❏ Parents staying unhappily married their whole lives
   - ❏ Parents divorcing during teenage years
   - ❏ Parents divorcing during childhood years
   - ❏ Parents separating but not divorcing
   - ❏ Parents divorcing and getting remarried
   - ❏ Parents splitting up and dating other people

3. Check the one statement that describes how you see your future marriage.
   - ❏ I plan to get married when I'm old enough.
   - ❏ I won't ever get married.
   - ❏ I'll only marry the right person for me.
   - ❏ I'll only marry once and that's it.
   - ❏ I plan on getting married, but I'll probably also get divorced.
   - ❏ I don't see what the big deal about marriage is.
   - ❏ I think it's better to live together before getting married.

4. Below are some responses kids have when their parents get divorced. Is each one a **G (good)** or **B (bad)** response?
   - ___ Avoid dealing with what is happening until they're older
   - ___ Try to find the positive side of what is happening
   - ___ Run away from home
   - ___ Actively try to figure out how to best deal with what is happening
   - ___ Keep their feelings to themselves
   - ___ Get mad at their parents and decide not talk to them
   - ___ Ask for help from people who care about them
   - ___ Try to get their parents back together again
   - ___ Say that they're going to move in with their best friend
   - ___ Ask God to help them respond to their parents' problems

5. How could each of the following Bible passages could help a teenager whose parents are splitting up or have divorced?
   Psalm 27:13, 14
   Psalm 68:5
   Romans 15:13
   2 Corinthians 4:8, 9
   1 Peter 1:3

"MY PARENTS SPLIT UP" [d i v o r c e]

THIS WEEK

This TalkSheet isn't about the right or wrong of divorce—or to judge those parents who may be split up or divorced. Teens aren't responsible for marital failure but they must live with its consequences.

Be sensitive to your group members who may be dealing with divorce or split families. There are many unique family situations today—even within the church. Pay close attention to the dynamics of your group and mediate this discussion.

OPENER

For this intro, you'll need five photocopies of a certificate (that kinda looks like marriage certificate), one frame, and some tape. Place one of the certificates into the frame, poke one with holes, tear one in several places, tear one into pieces and tape it back together again, and save one to be torn. Now hold the certificates up before the group. Explain that each of these certificates represents a marriage—

- The framed certificate is the picture-perfect marriage—the husband and wife care for each other and work hard at keeping the marriage together.
- The certificate with holes represents a marriage with some problems—there are a few difficulties eating away at it, but so far it's stayed together.
- The one torn in several places represents a hurting marriage—perhaps with help it will survive or it may end in divorce.
- The certificate torn into pieces but taped together again represents a marriage that has been torn apart but is healing—there are scars, but it can still last.
- Finally, the last certificate should be held up and torn to pieces. This represents a marriage that has ended in divorce—the certificate of marriage no longer means anything.

THE DISCUSSION, BY NUMBERS

1. What feelings did your group list? How are these different among kids whose parents aren't divorced? Be sensitive to those who don't want to share.

2. Use this question to let your kids share how they feel about their parents' marriages—do not use this to judge divorce. Do not allow put-downs of other family situations—each situation is unique.

3. How do your kids view marriage and divorce? Use this question to affirm the importance of marriage and the choices these young people will have with regard to their potential future marriages.

4. Young people have different ways of dealing

stress. Which of these responses are better than others? Why or why not? Talk about ways of dealing with parents, siblings, and parents' new dating partners.

5. What do these verses say that can help a teenager whose parents are divorcing or have divorced? What comfort do they have knowing that God understands and comforts them and their parents?

THE CLOSE

For a close, use this activity to illustrate the high divorce rate in today's society. Sit with your group in a circle so they can see you flipping a coin. As you flip the coin, have them call heads or tails. If they lose the toss, have them leave the circle. Continue this until everyone in your group has called a coin toss (or some of them, if your group is too big). Explain that this activity is like marriage and divorce—roughly half of all American marriages end in divorce. The people outside of the circle represent those whose marriages failed. You may want to mention that—statistically—if they marry again, their chance of another divorce is even higher.

What fears or questions do your kids have about divorce? What does God think about divorce? Remind them that no one is judging those who are divorce—only God knows and understands each situation. Encourage your kids to find an adult to talk with if they are angry at their parents—but point out that their parents need love and support, too. Close with a time of prayer for your kids and their families.

MORE

- You may want to assemble a group of four to five people for a panel discussion on divorce—for instance, a divorced person, an adult child of divorce, a Christian counselor or pastor, and a married couple. Have your group members write down their questions for the panel in advance if possible. What scares your group about marriage and divorce? How can they prepare themselves today for healthy marriages?

- Has the media influenced the divorce rate? Undoubtedly. You may want to take some time to talk about media influences with your kids. What do TV shows and movies say about divorce? What does music today say about divorce and splitting up? Does the media condone cheating on partners? How? Discuss each of these with your group and ask for specific examples that they may have.

DIFFERENT OR DISABLED?

1. Which age group do you feel has the most difficulty handling a **personal disability**?
   - ❑ Babies
   - ❑ Children
   - ❑ Teenagers
   - ❑ Young adults
   - ❑ Adults
   - ❑ Senior adults

2. Put an arrow ⇨ by the five conditions below that you know the most about.

Epilepsy	Learning disabilities	Paraplegia/quadriplegia
Diabetes	Speech impediments	Mental retardation
Amputation	Asthma	Learning disability
Deafness	Muscular dystrophy	Cleft palate or harelip
Obesity	Autism	Mental illness
Dwarfism	Multiple sclerosis	Other—
Cerebral palsy	Down's syndrome	
Blindness	Parkinson's disease	

3. Place an X alongside those conditions found in question 2 that you think kids at your school would be (or are) least accepting of.

4. Suppose you had one of the conditions listed above. Pick one and then answer these questions.
   How might people treat you if they saw you?

   How might you feel about yourself?

   If you were invited to a Christian youth group, how might you be treated?

   How would your life be different from others because of this condition?

5. The apostle Paul had a disability of some sort (2 Corinthians 12:7). In Galatians 6:11 the Bible gives a more specific hint regarding Paul's "thorn in the flesh." Paul says he pleaded with the Lord to take away this problem but the Lord had a different plan. Read God's plan for Paul and his disability in 2 Corinthians 12:9.

   How is a physical or mental challenge in today's world a chance to experience God's grace and power?

DIFFERENT OR DISABLED? [d i s a b i l i t i e s]

THIS WEEK

People with mental or physical challenges can scare or make junior highers or middle schoolers feel uncomfortable. Kids this age may not understand the condition and may be confused or frightened. And sometimes they make fun of people with disabilities to cope with their own fear and confusion. This TalkSheet offers the opportunity to discuss what it means to have a disability and a proper Christian response to these people.

OPENER

Write the following words on a whiteboard or poster board—defective, crippled, handicapped, afflicted, and deformed. What message do your kids get from each of these words? How do these words make them feel? Other words used to describe those with disabilities are the infirm, shut-in, and disabled. Your kids may have learned the proper terms in school—point out to the group that these individuals are people with disabilities or people who are physically or mentally challenged. What other names have your kids heard that unfairly describe those with disabilities? Have your kids seen, met, or known someone who has a disability? How does this affect their relationship with this person? Encourage your kids to be sensitive to the feelings of others, including those who are family members, relatives, or friends with someone who has a disability.

THE DISCUSSION, BY NUMBERS

1. Why might each age group have different difficulties? Discuss the myth that disability equals inability—which is simply not true. Point out, too, that another myth is that people with disabilities are unhappier than people without disabilities.

2. Many teenagers aren't informed about these conditions. So you may want to be prepared to define each of these. Information can go a long way in helping young people become more compassionate and caring.

   For more information on these conditions, check out the National Health Information Center (http://nhic-nt.health.org), The National Information Center for Children and Youth with Disabilities (http://nichcy.org), Christian Counsel on Persons with Disabilities (www.ccpd.org), or search any search engine with the keyword disabilities for hundreds of links to more information.

3. How can Christians influence others to be more accepting of those with disabilities? Ask the group to identify how the attitudes and actions of people without disabilities handicap people with disabilities.

Have the group identify the ways people with physical or mental challenges are like everyone else.

4. How would your kids handle these situations? How are the situations different based on the condition? What thoughts do your kid have for treating those with these disabilities?

5. The Lord's response to Paul is contrary to the thinking of our postmodern world. The world couldn't understand how power comes through weakness, yet that is God's message. God can work through disabilities to demonstrate his power. Additional Bible verses are Isaiah 40:31; 2 Corinthians 1:3, 4; and Ephesians 3:16, 17.

THE CLOSE

The following points can help you in wrapping up the session.

- People with disabilities are people.
- People with disabilities need to be treated with dignity and respect. Too often they're treated like objects. Others talk *for* them *or* at them, not *with* them.
- Disabilities like mental retardation aren't contagious. You don't catch them like the flu.
- Disability isn't the same as inability.
- Christ died for all people—because he loves all people, regardless of mental or physical abilities.
- Christ has called all Christians to be compassionate to these people.

How can your kids be more accepting and understanding of people with disabilities? What does God think about treating everyone equally?

MORE

● You may want to take your kids to a home for disabled persons. Possibly visit a nursing home or a hospital to play games, talk, and spend time with them. How did your kids feel while spending time with these people? What did they learn from these people? How did visiting help your kids understand disabilities?

● How does the media treat people with disabilities? How do TV shows or movies portray physical or mental disabilities? Why does the media and other people shy away from dealing with these issues? Why do advertisements show only the perfect, healthy people to sell their products? Why are there few TV show with disabled characters in them? What do your kids think about how the media handles these? Is it healthy for our culture or not? Does it help educate the public?

DOWN AND OUT

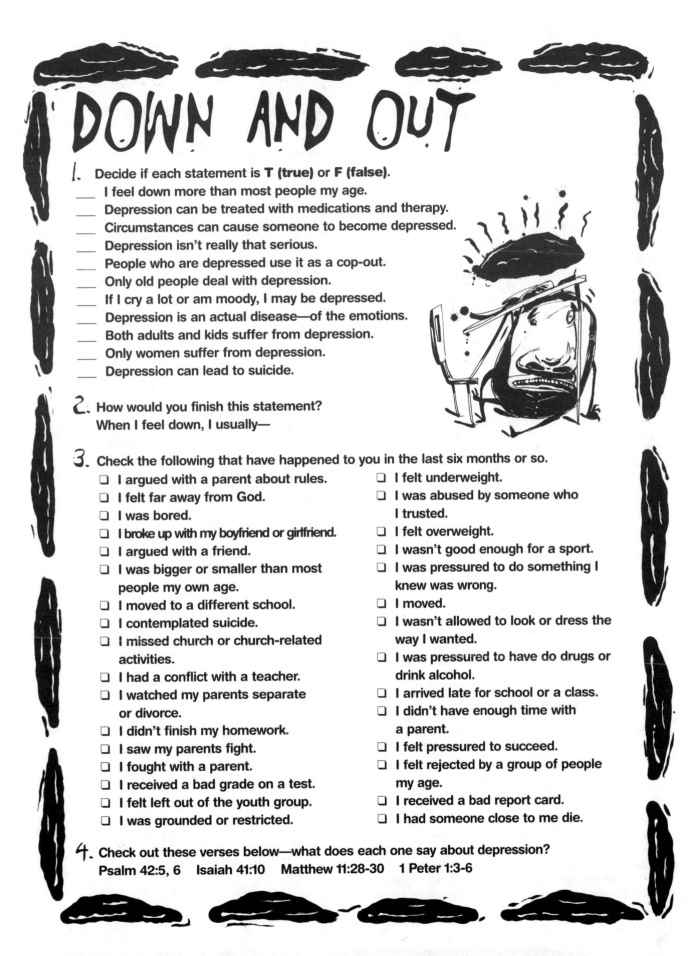

1. Decide if each statement is **T (true)** or **F (false)**.

___ I feel down more than most people my age.
___ Depression can be treated with medications and therapy.
___ Circumstances can cause someone to become depressed.
___ Depression isn't really that serious.
___ People who are depressed use it as a cop-out.
___ Only old people deal with depression.
___ If I cry a lot or am moody, I may be depressed.
___ Depression is an actual disease—of the emotions.
___ Both adults and kids suffer from depression.
___ Only women suffer from depression.
___ Depression can lead to suicide.

2. How would you finish this statement?
   When I feel down, I usually—

3. Check the following that have happened to you in the last six months or so.

❑ I argued with a parent about rules.
❑ I felt far away from God.
❑ I was bored.
❑ I broke up with my boyfriend or girlfriend.
❑ I argued with a friend.
❑ I was bigger or smaller than most people my own age.
❑ I moved to a different school.
❑ I contemplated suicide.
❑ I missed church or church-related activities.
❑ I had a conflict with a teacher.
❑ I watched my parents separate or divorce.
❑ I didn't finish my homework.
❑ I saw my parents fight.
❑ I fought with a parent.
❑ I received a bad grade on a test.
❑ I felt left out of the youth group.
❑ I was grounded or restricted.

❑ I felt underweight.
❑ I was abused by someone who I trusted.
❑ I felt overweight.
❑ I wasn't good enough for a sport.
❑ I was pressured to do something I knew was wrong.
❑ I moved.
❑ I wasn't allowed to look or dress the way I wanted.
❑ I was pressured to have do drugs or drink alcohol.
❑ I arrived late for school or a class.
❑ I didn't have enough time with a parent.
❑ I felt pressured to succeed.
❑ I felt rejected by a group of people my age.
❑ I received a bad report card.
❑ I had someone close to me die.

4. Check out these verses below—what does each one say about depression?
   Psalm 42:5, 6   Isaiah 41:10   Matthew 11:28-30   1 Peter 1:3-6

DOWN AND OUT [d e p r e s s i o n]

THIS WEEK

Young teenagers live on the edge of change—their bodies and minds are growing, their friend and family relationships are shifting, and they are facing new pressures, circumstances, and opportunities. These life circumstances cause kids to feel down and can lead to depression. Depression is a reality in today's society for both teenagers and adults.

It's crucial to know the facts about depression. Depression is a clinically diagnosed disease that affects millions of adults and teenagers each year. Be sensitive to your group members during this discussion and use this as an educational tool for them. And be sure to get the information you need before you start by checking out these Web sites—
- National Foundation For Depressive Illness, Inc. (www.depression.org)
- Depression Central(www.psycom.net/depression.central.html)
- Psychology Information Online (www.psychology info.com/depression/index.html)
- Depression.com (www.depression.com)
- Disorders and Treatments (http://depression.mentalhelp.net)

Or consider talking with a psychologist or doctor about depression and its effects.

OPENER

For a brief opener to this discussion, ask your kids what they think depression is. Some of them may have different ideas or misconceptions from the media. Make a master list of their ideas and the words they use to describe depression. Now ask them this question—how many kids their age suffer from depression? Have them take guesses at it. Then write down or read these facts to your group —
- Approximately four out of 100 teenagers get seriously depressed each year.
- Up to 20 percent of teenagers are diagnosed with some kind of mood disorder
- Depression can lead to suicide—the fifth leading cause of death among kids ages 5-14.

How does this information make your kids feel? Did they realize this information before? What does this information say about youth today and dealing with emotions and feelings?

THE DISCUSSION, BY NUMBERS

1. This question will give you a feel for what your kids know or understand about depression. Some may not know or understand what it is. Anyone, males and females, of any age can suffer from depression. It is more than feeling sad a lot, it's feeling down all the time—and it affects how a person's schoolwork, friendships, and physical health.

2. Create a master list of all the things that your group members do when they feel down. Split the list into healthy and unhealthy responses. What is the best solution for dealing with feeling down?

3. Let kids share the life events that have happened to them over the past six months. Point out that some of these events naturally cause people to feel down—and can trigger depression. Everyone has different personalities and react differently to events. How do your kids deal with these big changes? What are good and bad ways to deal with these changes?

4. Ask for volunteers to read these verses and try to apply them to today. What do these verses say about depression and feeling down?

THE CLOSE

Encourage your kids to listen to their friends when they experience low points of life. Both Elijah and Job had friends who supported them when they were down (1 Kings 19:19-21; Job 2:11-13). It's important to have a support network of family members, friends, teachers, or a youth pastor, who can encourage and support them.

Sometimes, feeling down turns into something more serious—clinical depression. These feelings of helplessness are powerful emotions that destroy lives, weaken relationships, and even lead to suicide (see links below). If any of your kids, their family members, or friends are dealing with feelings of depression, they must find professional help.

Finally, point out that depression and feelings of helplessness are not sinful. They're part of being human. Encourage your kids to find activities that help them feel better when they're down.

MORE

- You may want to talk about suicide with your group. What are some signs that your kids can look for in their friends or family members? Visit a few on-line organizations for more information—Suicide Voices Awareness of Education (www.save.org) and the American Foundation for Suicide Prevention (www.afsp.org). If there is a suicide hotline in your area, post the number for the kids to write down.
- Ask your kids pay attention to what they hear or see in the media on depression and suicide. Possibly show a short clip of a TV show of a teenage problem and discuss ways to handle the problem. How does the media portray suicide and depression? What TV shows or movies have they seen that addresses these issues? What have they read or seen on the issues of suicide and how teenagers handle their struggles?

THE AFTERLIFE

1. Write a word you think best describes **heaven** and a word you think best describes **hell**.
   Heaven—
   Hell—

2. What about you? Finish this statement.

   I think about heaven—
   ❑ Too much
   ❑ Too much
   ❑ Quite often
   ❑ Quite often

   I think about hell—
   ❑ Sometimes
   ❑ Sometimes
   ❑ Hardly ever
   ❑ Hardly ever

3. What do you think—do you **A (agree)** or **D (disagree)**?
   ___ Science has proven there is no heaven or hell.
   ___ People who live good lives will go to heaven.
   ___ Hell won't be as bad a place as preachers make it out to be.
   ___ It is easier to imagine a hell than a heaven.
   ___ Talking about hell will scare people into wanting to know more about how to go to heaven.
   ___ Christians should be more worried about the here and now rather than the afterlife.

4. What do you think life will be like in heaven?

5. The Bible doesn't tell us as much as we might want to know about heaven or hell. But it does say that both exist. The following verses give us a slice of what heaven and hell will be like. After each verse write a word or a phrase that describes either heaven or hell.

   Matthew 8:12
   Philippians 3:19
   2 Thessalonians 1:8, 9
   Revelation 21:8

   Psalm 123:1
   John 14:2
   Philippians 3:20, 21
   Revelation 21:4

THE AFTERLIFE [heaven and hell]

THIS WEEK

What do your kids think about heaven and hell? Most likely they've heard it talked about on TV, read about it in magazines, and heard about it in church. But all of these sources can be confusing to a junior higher or middle schooler. This TalkSheet will let you discuss both heaven and hell according to what the Bible says and what Christians believe.

OPENER

You may want to show some clips of a movie that portrays heaven or hell. Or ask your kids to brainstorm a list of movies and TV shows that have dealt with the afterlife. Need some suggestions? Try "What Dreams May Come" (PolyGram Films) and "Ghost" (Paramount Pictures). Also check out more movie reviews and summaries at http://www.christiananswers.net/spotlight/home.html and www.hollywoodjesus.com.

After you watch part of the movie, or talk with your kids about movies (or TV shows) they've seen, ask them a few questions. How did the characters deal with the subject of the afterlife? What happened in the movie? Do your kids think there are accurate representations of heaven or hell? Why or why not? What have your kids heard differently in church or in school? What is different and why?

THE DISCUSSION, BY NUMBERS

1. What words did your kids use to describe heaven and hell? Why did they pick the ones they did?

2. How often do your kids think about heaven or hell? Sometimes thinking about death and hell causes people to question the condition of their souls. What questions do your kids have about the afterlife? Many of them may have questions about reincarnation and other secular viewpoints that they have heard through friends or the media.

3. Do your kids agree or disagree? Take a poll on each of these issues and discuss each one. Ask the students to explain their views and give biblical support for their answers where appropriate.

4. What do your kids think it will be like to be with God? Where have they gotten their ideas?

5. The Bible does give glimpses of heaven and hell—and describes both as real places. Ask the group members to share their impressions of heaven and hell.

THE CLOSE

Heaven and hell are both a reality—the Bible tells us that both are real. God has given every person a choice—to love him and serve him, or not to. Your kids might ask why a loving God would condemn anyone to hell. But the real question is why would anyone want to reject God's love? God wants everyone to experience eternal life with him (John 5:24; 2 Peter 3:9). And each person is bound for one or the other (Ecclesiastes 12:13, 14). Point out that this lesson is not meant to scare them into believing in Jesus—but it is information that they should know. Let them know that you are willing to talk with them one-on-one if any of them have questions or other concerns.

MORE

- You might want to have your senior pastor and a few other adults come into the meeting to help answer the questions that your kids may have about heaven and hell. No one knows all the answers, but your group might like to hear outside ideas and ask questions, too.

- Have your kids split into groups and find more information on heaven and hell throughout the Bible. Give each group one of these verses—

Revelation 4:1-6	Revelation 21:15-21
Revelation 4:6-11	Revelation 21:22-27
Revelation 5:1-5	Revelation 22:1-5
Revelation 5:6-14	Matthew 8:12
Revelation 6:8	Luke 16:19-31
Revelation 7:16-17	Matthew 25:41
Revelation 19:1-10	2 Peter 2:4
Revelation 20:10-15	Jude 1:6
Revelation 21:1-8	2 Thessalonians 1:9
Revelation 21:9-14	Mark 12:25-27

Have your groups read these verses and then write down or summarize what each set of verses says about either heaven or hell. You may want to have volunteers read different verses out loud and then talk about the verses with your group. What new understanding of heaven or hell do they have?

THE HITS

1. List the different kinds of music that kids at your school listen to.

2. Do these statements describe you—**Y (yes)** or **N (no)**?

___ I listen to music because I like how it sounds.
___ The music I listen to makes me feel good.
___ I listen to music every day.
___ I think some types of music are more moral than others.

___ I read music magazines.
___ I watch music videos.
___ I have attended a music concert.
___ The lyrics of the music I listen to don't affect me.

3. What do you think—do you **A (agree)** or **D (disagree)**?
___ There's more good than bad in today's music.
___ Parents should have a say in the kind of music listened to by their kids.
___ Secular music is inspired by the devil.
___ Some types of music are worse than others.
___ Music has no affect on kids my age.
___ Adults shouldn't protect kids from secular music.
___ Secular music is a good source of information about life.
___ Today's concerts should be rated like movies.

4. What about your parents? Check which ones apply to you.

   a. I can talk with my parents about the songs I like.
      ❑ Every song
      ❑ Some songs
      ❑ No songs
   b. I can talk with my parents about the music videos I like.
      ❑ Every video
      ❑ Some videos
      ❑ No videos

   c. I would let my parents listen to the songs I like with me.
      ❑ Every song
      ❑ Some songs
      ❑ No songs
   d. I would let my parents watch the music videos I like with me.
      ❑ Every song
      ❑ Some songs
      ❑ No songs

5. Check out **Galatians 5:19-21** and write down which of the behaviors described could apply to today's music.

THE HITS [popular music]

THIS WEEK

Whether it is hip-hop, alternative, country, or rap—music is one phrase that defines youth culture today. It's become a medium targeted specifically at teenagers—who purchase over 125 million CDs a year*. But popular music—and the world it has created—has little or nothing to do with the home or church. Your junior highers or middle schoolers have already established listening habits. This TalkSheet has been designed to create a positive dialogue about popular, secular music between students and adult youth workers.

OPENER

Get some music that is completely different from what your kids listen to. Try to find some music from the 1930s and 1940s—or some classical music. Play the music as the young people arrive for your meeting.

What's their reaction to this music? How is this music different from what they listen to? How has music changed in youth culture? You may want to play a few more styles of music for them, too—maybe some oldies, some '70s disco, or '80s rock. What do your kids think of this music? Do they remember it? How has music changed over the years? How do your kids think music will continue to change over the years?

Or ask your group how music plays a role in everyday life—not just played on the radio. Where do your kids see music videos, hear music, or see music stars? Some of these include on TV advertisements, radio commercials, in movies, in stores, on billboards, and more. Discuss how music has invaded culture—in a good way—but the influences that it has. For example, what would a movie be like without a soundtrack? What would commercials be without background music?

THE DISCUSSION, BY NUMBERS

1. What kinds of music do are your kids' peers listening to? The responses to this question will give you an understanding of the diversity of bands that are popular with your kids.

2. How involved are your group members in the culture of popular music? Make a list of all of the positive things and negative things about some types of secular music. Encourage those who listen to primarily Christian music to share about why they like it—although sometimes it's hard to draw a line between Christian and mainstream.

3. Do your kids agree or disagree? What have your kids learned about love, life, God, hate, and so on from listening to popular music? Keep track of what they say on a whiteboard or poster board to help them see what values are promoted by today's popular music.

4. How much do your kids' parents know about the music they listen to and the music videos they watch? Would their parents be embarrassed by what their kids listen to? Why or why not? Can your kids involve their parents in helping them wise choices for music? Why or why not?

5. What does this verse say about listening to music? Read Galatians 5:22-23 and decide with your group how much mainstream music promotes the fruit of the Spirit.

THE CLOSE

Point out to your group that listening to popular music isn't bad. But some of the music they listen to is bad—the violent content, sexual themes, and other messages aren't good. (See Killer Tunes on page 99.) Be careful not to slam your kids with Bible verses or bash their favorite music groups. Instead focus on your kids' responsibility to choose the kinds of music they listen to wisely and to be discerning. Challenge your kids to choose songs that can keep their faith on Jesus and not worldly values. Ask your kids these questions—what happens to you when you listen to rap or hardcore metal? What Christian values do these songs ridicule? When you listen to this song, are you drawn closer or further away from God?

MORE

● With your group, brainstorm the values that most mainstream songs deal with. What are the themes that most talk about. These include love, drug abuse, violence, romance, suicide, and more. Make a list of these topics and values. Now ask your kids to guess what percentage of the music they listen to deals with these topics. On a scale of 1-10 (10 being the most applicable), how well does the music they listen to apply to their lives? Do they share the same values and morals that the musicians do? Why or why not? What influence do your kids think this has on them?

● Check out Plugged In magazine at www.family.org/pplace/pi/ (Focus on the Family) for the latest trends in music, TV, and movies. Check out www.YouthSpecialties.com for information and links to finding discussion topics and latest news on teen culture.

* Teen Fact Book 2000, Channel One Network: New York, Los Angeles, Chicago. Used by permission.

TALK IT THROUGH

FYI—the term parent in these questions refers to all kinds of parents—birth, step, foster, or guardian.

1. Which answer is most true for you?
   My parents and I talk about the really important things—
   - ❏ too much
   - ❏ about the right amount
   - ❏ not often enough

2. On a scale of 1-5 (1 being "we hardly ever talk" and 10 being "we talk all the time") how often do you talk about each of the following with one or both of your parents?

   ___ School grades
   ___ Internet
   ___ TV
   ___ Movies
   ___ Chores
   ___ Christian beliefs
   ___ Clothes and fashion
   ___ Your friends
   ___ Family rules
   ___ Alcohol or drugs

   ___ Your free time
   ___ Who you're going out with
   ___ Popular music
   ___ Church
   ___ Your responsibilities
   ___ Problems you have
   ___ Homosexuality
   ___ How your day went
   ___ Your family relationship
   ___ Sex

3. When you talk about each of the following with your mom or dad, how good are the discussions? **G (good discussion)**, **L (lecture)**, or **A (argument)**?

   ___ School grades
   ___ Secular music
   ___ Chores
   ___ Church
   ___ Boyfriends or girlfriends
   ___ Christian beliefs

   ___ Problems you have
   ___ Your friends
   ___ Family rules
   ___ Your responsibilities
   ___ Internet, TV or movies
   ___ Disobedience

   ___ Alcohol or drugs
   ___ How your day went
   ___ Sex
   ___ Your free time

4. Check out the following verses and summarize each one in your own words.
   Proverbs 15:1
   Proverbs 18:13
   Proverbs 20:3

   Proverbs 21:23
   Proverbs 29:20

TALK IT THROUGH [family communication]

THIS WEEK

Communication between parents and teenagers is important, but it doesn't happen enough. Parents fear they can't talk with their kids like they used to—kids wonder why their parents need to talk so much. Parents feel like they are running out of time to tell their kids all they will need to know—kids think they know it all. Use this TalkSheet time to examine the vital issue of communication and encourage more parent-teen dialogue.

OPENER

For this intro, write one of the following questions on a separate piece of paper (feel free to add more if you want).

- What would say to your mom or dad to get out of being grounded?
- What would you do if one of your parents wants to talk with you about sex?
- Describe the silliest talk you have ever had with a parent.
- If you could ask your parents any question and they would tell the truth, what question would you ask?
- How do you get money out of your parents when you need it?
- If you could talk with your parents about anything, and later they'd forget what was said—what would you talk or ask about?

Before your kids come in the room, tape a piece of paper under six different chairs. Or if your kids don't sit in chairs, put each of the six questions in an envelope and stick the envelopes around the walls of the room. When the group has sit down, ask them to either look under their chairs, or a nearby wall, for a question. Whoever finds the questions or envelopes has to read the question and answer it as best they can for the group.

THE DISCUSSION, BY NUMBERS

1. How often do your kids talk with their parents? Take a poll of where your kids see their communication on the important issues.

2. On a poster board or a whiteboard, write down which issues your kids talk with their parents about most often. Do the same for those issues that are rarely or never discussed. Ask the group members to summarize what this says about their overall communication with their parents.

3. Place the headings on the whiteboard or on a large piece of paper. Ask the group to share its responses, and keep track on the board. Discuss why certain topics seem to generally end up as lectures or arguments. What makes other topics easier to discuss?

4. What do these proverbs say about communication? Ask your students how they can apply these principles to the way they communicate with their parents.

THE CLOSE

You may have gotten a variety of responses from this discussion—some kids get along well with parents, but others can't stand their parents or the adults in their lives. Point out that communication with parents is important, and your kids can learn a thing or two. Encourage them to trust their parents—and give their parents a fair chance to communicate with them. After all, communication goes two ways (that's why it's called dialog!). Take time to discuss why your kids don't feel comfortable talking with their parents. What separates them? Why do some kids have better relationships with their parents than others? What can your kids do to hold up their end of the relationship? And point out that the Big Daddy upstairs is listening to them all the time—he's waiting for them to talk with him, too! Close with a time of prayer for your kids and their parents.

MORE

- Hold a talk show with your kids and some of their parents! You'll need four to eight parents as talk-show interview guests. Your group members will be the audience, and will ask questions or write down their questions in advance. Provide the host with two to three sample questions to start off the show. Here's a few suggestions—

⇨ What would you like to see teenagers talk with their parents about?

⇨ How often should parents and their kids sit down and talk?

⇨ Why aren't parents more understanding of their kids when they talk with them?

⇨ If you could tell young people only one thing about parents, what would it be?

- Unfortunately physical and sexual abuse happens within churched families. Encourage your kids to talk with a trusted adult— you or someone else. For more information on dealing with abuse, check out the National Exchange Club Foundation (www.preventchildabuse.com) or the American Humane Association (www.americanhumane.org), Rape, Abuse, and Incest National Network (www.rainn.org), The Family Violence Prevention Fund (www.fvpf.org), or Christians In Recovery (www.christians-in-recovery.com).

HOMOPHOBIA

1. Why are some kids called harsh names like **fag** or **queer**?

2. **Homophobia** means "fear of homosexuals". Check two reasons why teenagers might have homophobia. They might think—
   - ❏ Homosexuals are weird.
   - ❏ Homosexuals have a certain reputation.
   - ❏ Homosexuality is contagious.
   - ❏ Homosexuality is unfamiliar.
   - ❏ Homosexual behavior is a sin.
   - ❏ Homosexuals have AIDS.
   - ❏ Homosexuals hate God.
   - ❏ Homosexuals are usually bisexual.
   - ❏ Homosexuals might try to hit on you.
   - ❏ Other—

3. What do you think—**Y (yes)**, **N (no)**, or **M (maybe)**?
   - ___ Christians shouldn't talk about homosexuality.
   - ___ Homosexuals have the right to choose, just like heterosexuals.
   - ___ Heterosexual sex outside of marriage is just as much a sin as homosexual sex.
   - ___ Homosexuals are normal people, just like everybody else.
   - ___ Christians should be more loving toward homosexuals.
   - ___ Homosexuals should be quiet about their beliefs and sexual preferences.
   - ___ There isn't much that the church can do for homosexuals.
   - ___ Homosexuals need lots of prayer.
   - ___ There's nothing wrong with homosexuality.

4. What would you do if a homosexual sat next to you in church?

   Came up to you at school?

   Wanted to hang out with you?

5. What do each of these verses say about homosexuality?
   Leviticus 18:22
   2 Peter 3:9
   Romans 3:22 & 23
   1 John 4:15-18

HOMOPHOBIA [h o m o s e x u a l i t y]

THIS WEEK

Today's young people are growing up in a generation more tolerant of alternative lifestyles. The media tells teenagers that homosexuality is okay, portraying it regularly in movies and TV shows. Use this TalkSheet to discuss with your young people how Christians and the church can love the individual homosexual and hate the sin of homosexuality. Be sensitive to the fact that you may have kids in your group struggling with questions about this issue.

OPENER

Your kids most likely have seen homosexuality portrayed in movies and on TV. To start, ask your kids about homosexual characters they have seen in movies and on TV. You may want to make a master list of these shows and then ask your kids a few of these questions—

- What are these characters like? How are they portrayed in the movies or on TV?
- Are they primarily guys or girls? Why might one be shown more than the other?
- How the media stereotypes measure up to any gays or lesbians that your kids may know personally?
- How are homosexuals treated in movies and TV as opposed to how they are treated in real life?
- What does society—and the media—in general say about homosexuality?
- How is this the same or different from what the church believes?

THE DISCUSSION, BY NUMBERS

1. Your kids will also be able to give other labels of homosexuals, such as fairy, dyke, and butch. Be sure to maintain a level of respect while doing this activity—make sure that this does not turn into a contest to come up with the most slang terms or phrases for homosexuality. And keep your kids from making fun of homosexuality.

2. Point out that people label others because they fear and don't understand the other person. Encourage them to talk about their fears. Discuss the definitions of homophobe and homophobia. What are some everyday effects of these fears?

3. Discuss each of these statements, especially those that your kids don't agree on. Why do people have certain preconceptions about homosexuals? How can Christians demonstrate God's love to homosexuals?

4. How would your kids react in these situations? Why would some people react differently than others? Why do some people make such a big deal of being friends with homosexuals?

5. What do these verses say about homosexuality? How easy or difficult it is to hate the sin of homosexuality but love the sinner? How would Jesus have treated the homosexual?

THE CLOSE

Teenagers can have feelings for the same sex—even if they are for a moment. But this doesn't indicate the person is a homosexual. Some teenagers will experiment with homosexual behaviors. And they need God's forgiveness and grace just like teenagers who experiment with heterosexual behavior. This puts everyone in the same boat because everyone sins. Heterosexual sin is just as much a sin as homosexuality.

Some teenagers and adults persist in their homosexuality, claiming that it's genetically based or that they grew up in a dysfunctional, abusive family. Whatever the cause, homosexuals need to hear that Christ died for them and there are loving people in the church willing to help them with their sin struggle. The Bible clearly teaches that the act of homosexuality is a sin—a shameful and unnatural act—but Christ came to forgive sin and to love sinners.

MORE

- You may want to ask a group of parents to attend the session and talk about their views on the subject. Be sure to choose the parents carefully. It's important that they are respectful of homosexuals and the opinions of your kids. Encourage your group members to ask questions and debate the issue among themselves.

- Some of the kids in your group may have questions about homosexuality. Some of your kids may be involved in homosexual behaviors or have friends or family members who are homosexuals. If you need or would like more information to Christian links on this topic, check out Hope for Teens (www.hopeforteens.com), Exodus International North America (www.exodus-northamerica.org), National Association for Research and Therapy of Homosexuality (www.narth.com), Loving Grace Ministry, Inc. (www.lovinggraceministry.org), or Eagles' Wings Ministry (www.ewm.org).

SMUT WORLD

1. Check out these statements and decide if they're **T (true)** or **F (false)**.
   ___ Society does a good job of protecting kids my age from pornographic material.
   ___ Kids my age can get pornographic material easily.
   ___ Movies emphasize sex and nudity too much.
   ___ The Internet is an easy way to get pornographic material.
   ___ Kids my age aren't interested in pornography.
   ___ Child pornography is worse than adult pornography.
   ___ Reading a sexually graphic novel or book is the same as pornography.
   ___ Being hooked on pornography isn't any different than being hooked on sex.
   ___ Calling a sexual hotline (like a 900 number) can be pornographic.
   ___ Looking at pornographic material is a sin.

2. Would you **A (agree)** or **D (disagree)** with the statements below?
   ___ It's normal for kids my age to want to look at pornography.
   ___ More guys get hooked on pornography than girls do.
   ___ The more a person is exposed to pornography, the more that person will want to look at pornography.
   ___ Television programming contains visual material that could be considered pornographic.
   ___ Christians never get hooked on pornography.
   ___ If a person is exposed to sexually explicit material, he or she won't develop a healthy sexual outlook.
   ___ Internet pornography should be available to teens.
   ___ Magazines are the biggest resource for pornography.

3. On the line below, put an X where you think indicates how harmful pornography is on society.

   ◆ |||||||||||||||||||||||||||| ◆

   Hardly harmful at all   Extremely harmful

4. Circle which passage is the most helpful in dealing personally with the issue of pornography?
   1 Corinthians 10:11-13   2 Timothy 1:7
   Galatians 5:22-25   James 1:13-15
   Philippians 2:12, 13

SMUT WORLD [pornography]

THIS WEEK

In a culture saturated in sexuality, pornography is readily available to young teens—from bookstores to their home computer. Some sexually explicit material isn't defined as pornography, which is one reason it's so accessible to kids. And a lot of kids are hooked on it—leading to damaging relationships. Use this TalkSheet to discuss the issue of pornography with your group and to emphasize the harm of getting hooked on porn.

OPENER

Write these names and phrases on a whiteboard or poster board—

Internet porn sites	R-rated movies
Romance novels	NC-17 rated movies
Playboy or *Playgirl*	X-rated movies
Telephone 900 numbers	*Sports Illustrated*
Pornographic videos	Swimsuit Edition
Victoria's Secret catalog	

Now ask your kids to identify the top three ways students are introduced to pornography. They can add to the list you have created.

Be sure to review the ground rules found in the introduction of this book—confidentiality is key for this discussion. Many more young people than adults realize have been adversely affected by pornography.

THE DISCUSSION, BY NUMBERS

1. How did your kids respond to these statements? Take time to talk about the validity of these. How protected are your kids from porn? What sources are the most common for pornographic material?

2. As you go over these statements with your group, you may want to take a poll of their opinions. What were their reasons for each one?

   Remember to focus your discussion not on pornographic materials but on the attitudes and behaviors associated with pornography.

3. What statement did your kids agree or disagree with? What harm might come to the average teenager who has only casual exposure to pornography?

4. Which passages were most helpful in dealing personally with the issue of pornography? What might God say about your kids being involved in porn? How does this relate to sexuality and respect for others?

THE CLOSE

Remind your kids that pornography can seem harmless at first, but can be very dangerous. Help them understand that their initial exposure to pornography may seem innocent, but it can easily grow out of control. Being addicted to porn is like a drug—a serious addiction that ruins lives, alters relationships, and destroys marriages. It ruins a healthy view of sex and distorts the Christian view of love, commitment, and fidelity—it promotes promiscuity and exploits both men and women.

How can your kids deal with pornography in their own lives? How can they shield themselves from being exposed? What can they do if they are hooked already or have friends or family members who are? Encourage them to find help immediately—from a trusted adult, teacher, counselor, or you. And close with prayer with your group, asking for God's wisdom and strength to say no to the temptations all around them.

MORE

- You may want to ask a Christian counselor who is familiar with the addiction process and pornography to speak with your group. She or he can answer questions the young people have as well as discuss some case studies. Let the speaker know that you don't want to include graphic examples—you don't want to be pornographic in discussing pornography, but to talk about the pain and sorrow associated with the victims of pornography.

- For more information on dealing with pornography and helping your kids deal with these issues, check out these Web sites—eXXit (www.exxit.org), Breaking Free from Pornography (www.porn-free.org), Focus on the Family's resources (www.pureintimacy.org), or Caught By the Web (www.caughtbytheweb.com). These are Christian links—if you search for pornography in a general search engine, you may land up with some not-so-helpful links!

KILLER TUNES

1. Check the following words that describes music with a **violent message**.

   - ❑ Inspiring
   - ❑ Destructive
   - ❑ Rebellious
   - ❑ Emotional
   - ❑ Loud
   - ❑ Fun

   - ❑ Beneficial
   - ❑ Energetic
   - ❑ Annoying
   - ❑ Harmful
   - ❑ Violent
   - ❑ Anxious

2. What do you think bothers adults the most about violent lyrics?

3. Put an arrow by the phrases that describe what violent songs are about.

   Hurting others
   Racism is right
   Anger must be acted out
   Disobeying parents
   Drugs make everything better
   Anarchy is the answer
   Only care about yourself
   Do to other before they do to you
   Rape or molestation
   Religion is the source of all problems

   Life is meaningless
   Death is the solution
   Revenge will make you feel better
   Authority shouldn't be respected
   Girls are sex objects
   The police are corrupt
   Death and destruction now
   The occult is the new religion
   Control others with violence
   Hate others because they hate you

4. What do you think? Choose **Y (yes)**, **N (no)**, or **D (Duh! I don't know!)**.
   ___ Concerts with violent music should be off limits to kids younger than 15.
   ___ Violent lyrics don't have a harmful effect on kids.
   ___ Kids under the age of 12 shouldn't be allowed to listen to violent music.
   ___ Violent songs should be rated like movies.
   ___ Kids who listen to violent music are more likely to get into trouble than kids who don't.
   ___ Teenagers should be allowed to listen to whatever kind of music they want.

5. Check out **Colossians 2:8** and complete this statement in your own words.
   One thing about violent music that could lead a person away from Christ is—

KILLER TUNES [violent music]

THIS WEEK

Young teens today are exposed to more violent music than before—much of it pushed by harder and more violent themes. The angry lyrics come in various kinds—gangster rap, alternative, hardcore, grunge, punk, and so on. This TalkSheet offers the opportunity to discuss these forms of violent music, which are having a profound influence on young people.

OPENER

You may want to arrange to have a music CD that has violent, angry lyrics playing as group members arrive. Observe their reactions. Were they annoyed, excited, or ignoring the music? Then point out the reactions to the group. How did the music make them feel? Were they surprised to hear the music here? Why or why not?

Ask your kids to name some bands that promote violence with their lyrics. Make a list of these groups. Which ones are popular with kids at their school? What do their lyrics promote—drugs, alcohol, sex, abuse, rape? How do your kids think this music influences people? Do they notice a difference in the kids at school who listen to this music and those who don't? What are the differences? Do they act differently, more violently? Why or why not?

THE DISCUSSION, BY NUMBERS

1. Ask the kids to share their words, and by doing so, your group is defining violent music. See if your group can decide if there is something about the melodies, as well as the lyrics, that makes these songs so distinctly violent.

2. What bothers your kids about this music? Give them time to talk, but don't let the sharing turn into a gripe session. Be careful not to condemn the music—condemning the music as satanic (or whatever) isn't a solution. Let your kids be heard and affirm their responses. But point out the influences that the music has.

3. Take this time as an opportunity to discuss the lyrical content of these songs. Keep the discussion general to avoid being offensive. You may want to read some lyrics from a CD to point out the graphic and violent nature of the songs.

4. Take time to explore each of these statements. If the students believe the violent music has an affect on young people, ask them for specific examples. Discuss when students should have total control over what they listen to and why—most usually give their ages as the appropriate age. What do they think about rating music like movies? Do parental advisory warnings help? Why or why not?

5. Make a list of all the things your group members identified. Is listening to this music a sin? Is it a sin if it leads to violent or harmful thoughts or actions? How can Satan use these types of music to pull Christians away from God?

THE CLOSE

Young teens usually have well-established music listening habits. But as they get older, they'll be exposed to more violent and sexually explicit music. Point out to your kids that they don't have to be passive receptors of any of this music—they do have a choice. Encourage your kids to be discerning with the kinds of music that they chose to listen to. And let them know that they can be influenced by these kinds of music—music is powerful. How can your kids get closer to God and be influenced by this music at the same time? Probably not going to happen. Discuss ways to deal with this issue.

One of the strongest impacts you can have on your group is to simply summarize the points made during the discussion. Some of your kids may like their violent music, but if you listened and respected the opinions of all participants, most group members will have openly talked about the negative aspects of such music.

MORE

- You may want to have your kids bring in their favorite CDs. Or find a music magazine or catalog (like BMG or Columbia House) to look at with your group. Pick out some different artists and styles of music and read the description of a CD or some lyrics from inside. With your group, create a standard for rating the CDs like movies are rated (G, PG, PG-13, R, NC-17). Then rate the CDs and discuss the reasons why each was given the rating it received.

- If you want to take this discussion further, talk about the influences of violent music on people. Focus on satanic music and the influences of music that promote rape, sexual abuse, physical abuse, drug abuse, alcohol abuse, hatred, and more. How does this music cause kids to swear more, become more violent, or change their relationships with others? For more information on music and reviews (both Christian and non) of all kinds of music, check out Plugged In Magazine (www.family.org/pplace/pi), Billboard (www.billboard-online.com/reviews), CD Shakedown (www.cdshakedown.com), MTV (www.mtv.com), or Wall of Sound (http://wallof-sound.go.com/reviews).

HEART TO HEART TALK

1. Check the one prayer pattern listed below that describes you.
   - ❑ I hardly ever pray.
   - ❑ I pray but usually only at church or before meals.
   - ❑ I pray more than just at church and before meals.
   - ❑ I pray quite a bit.
   - ❑ I pray all of the time.

2. How satisfied are you with your prayer life?
   - ❑ It's cool.
   - ❑ It needs some improvement.
   - ❑ It stinks.

3. **Y (Yeah)** or **N (nope)**? Have you ever—
   - ___ Wondered if God was really listening when you prayed?
   - ___ Felt especially close to God while praying?
   - ___ Wondered if God really answers prayer?
   - ___ Received an answer to a prayer request?
   - ___ Not wanted to pray, but did so anyway?
   - ___ Wanted to pray, but didn't know what to say?

4. Would you consider these statements to be **T (true)** or **F (false)**?
   - ___ People who pray are generally happier than people who don't pray.
   - ___ People who pray are better Christians that those who don't.
   - ___ Prayer is a way to strengthen relationships with God and others.
   - ___ God listens to some people's prayers more than others.
   - ___ People can pray any time, anywhere—God always listens.
   - ___ If I think my prayer might sound dumb, I won't pray.
   - ___ God listens to adult prayers more than kids prayers.

5. Read **Hebrews 4:14-16** and write down one new thing you learned about prayer.

HEART TO HEART TALK [prayer]

THIS WEEK

Prayer is an essential part of the Christian life! Your kids need to be encouraged to talk—and to listen—to God. Despite the importance of prayer, many teenagers spend very little time doing it, for a number of reasons. Maybe they don't know how to pray or what to ask for, or doubt if God listens. Use this TalkSheet to discuss prayer, its role in Christian growth, and how it brings people closer to God.

OPENER

Hand out a paper lunch bag, some small pieces of paper, a marker, and a pen or pencil to each member of the group. If you have a big group, you can split it into smaller groups and give each group a paper bag. Have your group members write prayer requests, short prayers, thanks, or anything else they'd like to say to God on some pieces of paper. Then have them put these papers inside the paper bags.

Now have each person (or group leader) write the word HEART on the outside of the paper bag. Point out that the bag represents each group member's heart. And inside is their thoughts and requests. Explain that God knows each person's heart and what's on their heart—including their fears, anxieties, sorrows, and joys. He is their friend and he wants to help them with their struggles and worries. Prayer comes from the heart and God knows their hearts.

Tell the kids (or group leaders) to hang on to the bags until the end of the discussion.

THE DISCUSSION, BY NUMBERS

1. You may want to take a poll to determine a group average. If your kids don't want to share, that's okay. Maybe have a few volunteers share their answers. Then use this item to evaluate how much your kids pray and why or why not.

2. Are your kids satisfied with their prayer lives? Why or why not? What keeps them from praying more? What can they do to pray more?

3. What have your kids wondered about? What questions do they have about prayer? How they answered these statements will give you a good indication of where they're at. Encourage them to ask questions.

4. As a follow-up to question 3, how did your kids react to these statements? What were the true and false statements? Why or why not?

5. Ask for volunteers to share what they learned

about prayer. You may want to let the kids use a Bible concordance to look up additional passages about prayer.

THE CLOSE

To close, you can do a few different things with the bags from the opener—

- Collect the bags and make a list of all the prayer requests and praises. You can filter through them to see which ones are too personal to share with the group. Then pray together as a group, either with one prayer leader or popcorn style.
- Have your kids pull out the papers that they'd like to share with the group or pray about. Collect those and make a list of these prayer requests and other items to pray about.
- Let your kids keep their bags for prayer on their own. Then give them time to spread out in the room and pray to God alone, going through the papers in the bag and bringing those requests to God.

Either way, point out that writing down prayer requests, praises, and so on helps a person pray. Especially for those who don't know what to say to God. But prayer is a conversation between a person and God. Encourage your kids to find a prayer style that's comfortable for them and to set a goal for their prayer life—maybe to pray everyday for a short time, to pray a certain time during the day, or whatever works for them. The closer they come to God, the closer he'll come to them (James 4:8).

MORE

- Your youth group activities calendar can double as a prayer calendar. The next time you create your calendar, write the names of kids and adults involved in your group in each of the daily squares. Point out to your kids that on different days can pray for the specific person listed. Hand out the calendars and encourage your students throughout the month to keep up their prayer support for members of the youth group. Later follow up with them to see how the activity worked and why or why not.
- What's God's model for prayer? Check out the Lord's Prayer with your group. Break it up into sections and give each small group a phrase of the Lord's Prayer. Ask them to discuss what the section of prayer means and then write it in their own words. Then together as a group, put all the sections of the prayer together and write a master group interpretation of the Lord's Prayer.

WHITE LIES AND OTHER HALF-TRUTHS

1. What was the **worst thing** that happened to you because you lied?

2. Who do you lie (or have you lied) to the most?

3. What do you think—**Y (yes)** or **N (no)**?
   ___ Boys lie more often than girls do.
   ___ It's easier to tell the truth than to lie.
   ___ It's easier to lie than to tell the truth.
   ___ You can get more from lying than from telling the truth.
   ___ Most lies don't hurt anyone.
   ___ There's a difference between a white lie and a big lie.
   ___ Lying is a sin just like any other sin.
   ___ There are times when a teenager has to lie.

4. How right or wrong are each of the following lies? **V (very wrong)**, **W (wrong)**, **S (semi-wrong)**, or **A (all right)**?
   ___ You lie to your parents about finishing homework to get them off your back.
   ___ You lie to your friend's parents to keep the friend from getting into trouble.
   ___ You lie to your boyfriend or girlfriend about cheating on him or her.
   ___ You lie yourself into an Internet chat room.
   ___ You lie to a teacher so that you'll be given an extra day to finish a report.
   ___ You lie to your parent about where you've been so you won't get into trouble.
   ___ You lie to a friend to avoid hurt feelings.
   ___ You lie about your age to get into a movie theater.
   ___ You lie to a stranger about where you live.

5. Read the five verses below and connect them to the matching phrases.
   Then cross out the extra one.

   a. Exodus 20:16
   b. Psalm 5:9, 10
   c. Proverbs 12:22
   d. Proverbs 19:9
   e. Colossians 3:9

   1. The Lord hates it when we lie, but he loves honesty.
   2. God approves of lying when you have to do it.
   3. One of the Ten Commandments says not to lie.
   4. Some people are full of deceit.
   5. Christians are brand new people who do not need to lie.
   6. Bad stuff happens when you lie.

WHITE LIES AND OTHER HALF-TRUTHS [lying]

THIS WEEK

Young teenagers lie—and many of them lie often. Some lie for different reasons which seem okay to them. But this pattern of lying that appears to be a culturally acceptable isn't part of God's plan for living. Use this TalkSheet discussion time to talk about the lying.

OPENER

Start by asking the group the following questions—if you were to be hooked up to a lie detector, would you agree to answer any question your parents asked you? How about any question your youth pastor asked you? Your best friend? Your boyfriend or girlfriend? Would some questions be harder to answer honestly than others? How do they feel knowing that God already knows all their answers?

Or you may want to talk about ways that lying is considered good or bad. Make a master list of their reasonings. For example, girls might think it's okay to lie to a strange man who is asking them personal questions. What are some other examples of situations? What would be other ways to handle these situations besides just lying? How does the media portray lying? Does it condone it as good or bad? Necessary? How has this altered the black and white of lying?

THE DISCUSSION, BY NUMBERS

1. Let some of your group members share their experiences. What were the consequences of their lies? How did these situations turn out? Point out that the negative consequences of lies outweigh any positive benefits.

2. The majority of teenagers lie most often to their parents. Ask the group who teenagers in general lie to the most. Why or why not? Why do people lie to the people that are closest to them, such as parents, loved ones, and God?

3. Discuss each statement asking for volunteers to share their answers. Point out that lying gives the deceptive feeling of control and power, but this feeling is an illusion. And it often backfires in the end.

4. Use this activity to talk about how people rationalize and justify lying. Why do people believe that their good intentions are reason enough to lie? Point out that God looks at the big picture. How do they know that their intentions are so good? How can they be sure that their lies will ensure that everything will work out?

5. Ask the young people to read the passages and match them up correctly. Discuss the verses one at a time and ask the kids to try to apply their messages to their own lives.

THE CLOSE

Point out that lying causes a lot of damage because it breaks trust. And those who lie—and get away with it—find it easier to lie than to tell the truth, especially in a sticky situation. It's addictive to some people that way. But lying can lead to big problems, especially with people who are close to them. Point out that Satan (the "father of lies") lied to Eve about the fruit in the Garden of Eden, which eventually lead to the fall of mankind.

God straight-out says that lying is wrong. Take some time to talk about this with your kids in light of the opening activity. Remind them that God is faithful, and that he loves them and forgives them. Encourage them to get right with God and others who they've hurt by lying. And challenge them to make honesty their number one goal from now on.

MORE

- If you have a high level of trust must exist within your group, try this activity. Remind your kids of the TalkSheet ground rule about confidentiality and group trust. Then ask your kids to share one lie that they wish they could erase and why. Jumpstart this activity by telling them one of your lies. Help your kids to appreciate the benefits of honesty and wrap up by talking about these.
- You may want to talk more about how lying affects trust and respect in relationships. How can lying hurt a friendship, a relationship with a boyfriend or girlfriend, or relationships with parents? What happens when someone is caught lying? What happens when someone lies to police, judges, or other officials? What does lying say about respecting oneself and others?

THE JOY FACTOR

1. **How happy are you today?**
   - ❏ Very happy
   - ❏ Happy
   - ❏ Sort of happy
   - ❏ Not too happy
   - ❏ Not happy at all

2. You have just won $100,000.00. What could you possibly buy that would make you happy?

3. What brings you happiness? Check off your **top three** choices.
   - ❏ A purpose in life
   - ❏ Salvation
   - ❏ Good looks
   - ❏ Helping others
   - ❏ Athletic ability
   - ❏ Material things
   - ❏ Good grades
   - ❏ Money
   - ❏ Health
   - ❏ Eating good food
   - ❏ Positive family life
   - ❏ Boyfriend or girlfriend
   - ❏ Popularity
   - ❏ Relationship with Christ
   - ❏ Great friends
   - ❏ Other—

4. How would you finish this statement?
   I would be happier if—

5. Which one is true for you?
   My relationship with Christ is important to my happiness.
   - ❏ All of the time
   - ❏ Some of the time
   - ❏ None of the time

6. Check out the verses below and match the references with the statements on the right.
   - a. Psalm 1:1
   - b. Psalm 32:1, 2
   - c. Proverbs 3:13
   - d. Proverbs 16:20
   - e. John 15:11
   - f. Philippians 4:4

   1. Joy is complete in Christ.
   2. God forgives our sins.
   3. Rejoice in the Lord.
   4. Stay away from evil.
   5. Trust in the Lord.
   6. Wisdom is a blessing.

THE JOY FACTOR [h a p p i n e s s]

THIS WEEK

More than any other age group, young people indicate their desire to be happy—but do they know what they want? What brings them happiness and why? This TalkSheet discusses happiness versus joy and Christianity versus the world's understanding of happiness.

Some of your kids aren't happy at all—they may be dealing with issues such as divorce, abuse, depression, failing grades, break ups, and more. Use this activity to talk about what brings happiness and how God can strengthen and fill them with his love and joy.

OPENER

What makes your kids happy? Start by having your kids write down what makes them happy. Let them know that you're going to use these for a game, so to keep their thoughts to themselves. Have them write as many as they can and then collect them (and check them over for inappropriate suggestions). Then use these as items for a round of Pictionary. Split your group up into teams with a drawer for each team. Have him or her draw an item for the rest of the group. The group gets a point if they can guess the topic. If not, another team gets a chance to guess. Play until each the items are gone and each team has drawn equally. The team with the most points wins.

THE DISCUSSION, BY NUMBERS

1. Get a consensus to figure out how they are feeling. You may want to let kids explain their personal ratings and why they're feeling a certain way. Be sensitive to those kids who are hurting and aren't happy. And mediate this discussion so it doesn't become too big of a gripe session.

2. Point out that people find happiness by things that can be bought. Many people spend a lifetime trying to buy happiness. Why would this money make your kids happy? Why not? What would they buy and why? Why do they think our society equates money as happiness?

3. Put the list on the whiteboard or poster board and then ask the group to identify the top five or so items that people their age would say brings happiness. Now ask the group to share those that they checked. Was there a difference between the average kid and your kids? Why or why not? Is there a difference between those who are and aren't Christians? Which of the things on the list are worth building one's life around?

   Point out that the things that make life worth

living are things that bring happiness. If people spend their lives pursuing happiness—which is called hedonism—they won't find it.

4. Often people play the "if only" game, thinking that a thing or a circumstance will make them happy. Ask the kids if this has been true in their lives.

5. Explore how a relationship with Christ brings happiness (John 15:9-17). Why are some Christians unhappy? How does happiness differ from God's joy (a fruit of the Spirit)?

6. How do each of these verses apply to happiness in today's world? You may want to read each of these verses and discuss this further.

THE CLOSE

Happiness is conditional, but joy—given by God's Spirit—brings happiness, even in times of doubt, pain, worry, and struggle. Paul, writing to the Philippians, said he had learned to be content with plenty or with little. He could live through either circumstance through the strength given by Christ (Philippians 4:11-13).

What do your kids need to do to find God's joy? Pray more? Get closer to him? Talk with an adult or pastor to learn more? Repent of some sin? Get right with their friends or parents? Encourage your kids to find what is making them discontent and to fix it, with God's help.

MORE

● Are your kids dealing with the pain of divorce, depression, guilt, and more? Spend some time talking about these with your group and encourage them to find someone to talk to—including you—who they feel comfortable with. For more information and links, see these TalkSheets—Got Faith? (page 29), Hooked on Drugs (page 35), Sexual Stuff (page 13), Too Much Too Soon (page 73), "My Parents Split Up" (page 83), and Down and Out (page 87).

● You may want to take some time to look more in depth at Paul's life. What a life this guy had! He was converted by becoming blind, had a "thorn in the flesh", endured a shipwreck, numerous floggings, and more. Read some chapters on Paul's life in Acts and discuss them with your group. How did Paul handle these situations? How can these be an example for our lives today? What does Paul's life say about God's faithfulness and love?

BLOCKBUSTERS

1. What types of movies do you watch the most, either at home or in the theater? Circle your top three choices.

Adventure
Action
Cartoon
Comedy
Drama

Family
Romance
Horror
Musical
Science fiction

Sports
Blood and gore
Western
Black and white classics

2. You're the movie critic! Using the rating system found in the box below—and using your own beliefs and rating system—rate two movies you recently watched at the theater or at home.

> **Movie Rating Guidelines**
> G (General Audience)
> PG (Parental Guidance Suggested)
> PG-13 (Parent Caution)
> R (Restricted)
> NC-17 (No One Under 17 Admitted)

Movie:
Rating—
Reason for the rating—

Movie:
Rating—
Reason for the rating—

3. How old do you think kids should be before making their own movie viewing decisions?

4. You're sleeping over at your friend's house when your friend's dad comes in the door with a rented R-rated movie. You know you're not supposed to watch the movie (legally, because you're under 17, but also because your parents would kill you), but everyone else wants to see it.

What will you do?

What will you tell your parents later?

What does this say about your friend's dad?

5. What does **Philippians 4:8 & 9** have to say about movies?

BLOCKBUSTERS [m o v i e s]

THIS WEEK

Watching movies is a common thing to do, whether it's by renting a video on a Saturday night or going out to the theater. Cable, VHS, and DVD movies allow junior highers and middle schoolers to watch nearly anything whenever they want—regardless of rating. And today's movie rating guidelines mean less and less—what was once rated X now qualifies as an R or even a PG-13 movie. This TalkSheet provides you with the opportunity to talk about the kinds of movies your group members are viewing—in an educational, nonjudgmental way.

OPENER

Start by getting a list of movies showing in your town (from a newspaper or off the Internet). Write their names on a poster board or whiteboard. Your kids will most likely know all the titles and may even have seen a few. Ask your kids to see if they can guess how each movie is rated. How close do they come? Write the rating next to the movie title. Point out that so often people don't even look at the ratings before going to the movie. What are the ratings for? How many of their parents enforce the ratings? Why are certain movies rated the same as others, but have less violent or sexual content?

For information on movies and reviews, check out www.HollywoodJesus.com, Preview Family and Movie Review (www.gospelcom.net/preview), Plugged In Magazine (www.family.org/pplace/pi), or Movie Guide (http://movieguide.crosswalk.com/main), Movie Finder (www.moviefinder.com), or Film.Com (www.film.com).

THE DISCUSSION, BY NUMBERS

1. Ask the group members to share the names of several movies from each of their top three choices. This will give you a picture of the kinds of movies your kids are viewing. In order to get a parental perspective, ask the group how many of the movies they've watched would meet their parents' approval.

2. This activity will (1) help kids become more aware of the reason for a rating system, (2) help kids discern good from bad moral content, and (3) will help kids create their own Christian rating system. Ask the group to create a list of all the reasons for rating a movie NC-17, R, PG-13, PG, and G. You will get answers like violence, foul language, sex, nudity, and so on. Now challenge the kids to create their own rating system in light of Christianity. How would they rate the movies differently?

3. Usually kids choose their own age as an appropriate age for a kid to make their own movie viewing decisions. Since many of the kids will say they're ready to make their own decisions, ask them if they are making good or bad decisions and why.

4. A common problem faced by parents today is the VCR or DVD player that belongs to their kid's friend. Some families (both Christian and non) have adopted much more liberal viewing rules than other families. The dilemma that kids face is how to keep their friends while maintaining their Christian stands and abiding by their parents' rules. Use this attention-getter to discuss this pressure faced by today's kids. See if the group can come up with several solutions to the dilemma.

5. Let several of the group members share what they believe this passage says about movies. Compare this verse with the rating system the group created for question 2.

THE CLOSE

Let the kids know that they do have decisions to make when it comes to going to the theater or watching a movie at home. Just because a movie was made doesn't mean that it should be seen. Challenge your kids to find out about the movies before they see them (possibly refer them to one of the sites listed above). Encourage them to be discerning with what they see and to take responsibility for their parents' rules and their own beliefs.

MORE

- You can use movies to teach your youth! Check out *Videos That Teach* by Doug Fields and Eddie James (Youth Specialties). This book includes over 75 teachable movie moments from film classics on over a hundred topics. Also, visit the Web site www.teachwithmovies.org for ideas on teaching with movies.
- Consider going to a movie or watching a video with your kids. Make sure that it's a rating that passes the approval of all parents. Afterwards talk about the movie in light of Christianity and their beliefs. What was the movie about? What message did it give about life, love, and happiness? What good or bad influences could this movie have on others? Why or why not?

LOVE AND FEAR IN THE TIME OF AIDS

1. Where have you learned about AIDS? Check all that apply.
   - ❑ Magazines
   - ❑ Parents or guardians
   - ❑ Teachers
   - ❑ TV shows
   - ❑ Movies
   - ❑ Celebrities
   - ❑ On the news
   - ❑ Internet
   - ❑ Friends
   - ❑ Boyfriends or girlfriends
   - ❑ Pamphlets
   - ❑ Church
   - ❑ Other peers at school

2. Do you agree with this statement? Why or why not?
   AIDS makes sex scary.

3. Check two of the statements below. When kids your age hear about AIDS, what do they think?
   - ❑ They shouldn't touch anyone with AIDS.
   - ❑ They're afraid to get AIDS.
   - ❑ They should make fun of those with AIDS.
   - ❑ They want to help someone with AIDS.
   - ❑ They feel sorry for a person with AIDS.
   - ❑ There's a cure for AIDS.
   - ❑ They want to know more about AIDS.
   - ❑ They're not really worried about it.

4. Drew was recently diagnosed with AIDS, most likely from a blood transfusion he received during his emergency surgery. The doctor said he's healthy enough to attend school and church.
   Would you want Drew to attend your school?

   Would you want Drew to attend your church?

   Would you want to be the same cabin with Drew at summer camp?

   Would you want to be close friends with Drew?

5. Decide how each of the following passages can be applied to the issue of AIDS.
   Mark 1:40, 41
   Romans 8:35-39
   Romans 12:2
   2 Corinthians 1:3-10
   Revelation 21:4

LOVE AND FEAR IN THE TIME OF AIDS [A I D S]

THIS WEEK

What do your kids know about AIDS? What misconceptions have they gotten from their parents, teachers, friends, the media, or the church? Although they've heard about it from school, it's important to discuss AIDS and how it relates to Christianity, their beliefs, and the church at large.

OPENER

Place the following bold terms on a whiteboard or poster board. Ask the kids to explain what these terms mean. Where have they heard these terms talked about before?

- **Abstinence**—To say no to something. When referring to the AIDS virus, the safest way to avoid the disease is to abstain from premarital sex and drug use.
- **AIDS**—A severe disorder of the immune system caused by the retrovirus HIV.
- **Hemophilia**—A disease of the blood that requires people to get blood transfusions and blood clotting products. Since AIDS can be transmitted through the blood, some hemophiliacs have contracted the disease through transfusions.
- **Heterosexual**—A person who is sexually attracted to members of the opposite sex. Heterosexuals can get AIDS just as homosexuals can.
- **HIV**—human immunodeficiency virus is the virus that causes AIDS.
- **Homosexual**—A person who is sexually attracted to members of the same sex. Homosexuals have been at high risk for getting AIDS because of their often risky sexual behavior, but AIDS isn't a homosexual disease.
- **Immune system**—That part of the body that protects us from disease. AIDS attacks this part of the body so that it cannot fight off other diseases.
- **Intravenous drug user**—A person who takes drugs with a needle. IV drug users often share needles, which spreads the AIDS virus.
- **Kaposi's sarcoma**—A rare type of cancer that people with AIDS frequently get.
- **Monogamous**—A faithful sexual relationship with only one other person.
- **STD**—A sexually transmitted disease that can be given to someone through sexual contact. AIDS is one of many STDs.

THE DISCUSSION, BY NUMBERS

1. Explore with the students what they have learned and already know about AIDS. Where have they gotten the majority of this information? Has the info been true or not? What misconceptions does the media give about AIDS and those who have it?

2. Ask the group to explain its answers. Some young people have different views of sex because they've experienced or heard about sexual abuse, rape, and AIDS.

3. Discuss the group's answers, then talk about a Christian response to those with AIDS. Point out how Christ had compassion for those with leprosy. How does the church treat those with AIDS? How about kids at school and their friends?

4. Talk about some of the myths associated with AIDS. The following are facts that kids need to know.
   - You can't get AIDS from casual contact like shaking hands.
   - Safe sex is not absolute. The best way to avoid contracting the disease is to abstain from premarital sex.
   - You can't recognize someone who has AIDS simply by looking at them.
   - AIDS isn't a punishment from God for sexual sin.
   - People can get AIDS from blood transfusions and other ways, besides having sex.

5. Ask several volunteers to share their opinions. What do these verses say about AIDS and how to treat those with AIDS?

THE CLOSE

Review the points made during the discussion and point out that those people with AIDS are just like everyone else. AIDS is a disease, just like cancer or any other disease—it's not a curse from God. Christians need to take God's love to people who have AIDS or any other disease. And it's important to realize that AIDS isn't associated just with homosexuality—many heterosexuals and children are living with or have died of it. Christ died for all people and loves them equally—either with or without AIDS.

MORE

- You can get more information on AIDS from your local Red Cross or public health department. Or check the American Foundation for AIDS Research (www.amfar.org), HIV/AIDS Treatment Information Service (www.hivatis.org), AIDS Research Information Center (www.critpath.org/aric), or Stop Aids Now (www.silcom.com/~stopaids).
- AIDS is just one of many sexually transmitted diseases. Are your kids familiar with other STDs? Find some facts on STDs or visit CDC National Prevention Information Network (www.cdcnpin.org) or the American Social Health Association (www.ashastd.org).

RESOURCES FROM YOUTH SPECIALTIES

YOUTH MINISTRY PROGRAMMING

Camps, Retreats, Missions, & Service Ideas (Ideas Library)
Compassionate Kids: Practical Ways to Involve Your Students in Missions and Service
Creative Bible Lessons from the Old Testament
Creative Bible Lessons in 1 & 2 Corinthians
Creative Bible Lessons in John: Encounters with Jesus
Creative Bible Lessons in Romans: Faith on Fire!
Creative Bible Lessons on the Life of Christ
Creative Bible Lessons in Psalms
Creative Junior High Programs from A to Z, Vol. 1 (A-M)
Creative Junior High Programs from A to Z, Vol. 2 (N-Z)
Creative Meetings, Bible Lessons, & Worship Ideas (Ideas Library)
Crowd Breakers & Mixers (Ideas Library)
Downloading the Bible Leader's Guide
Drama, Skits, & Sketches (Ideas Library)
Drama, Skits, & Sketches 2 (Ideas Library)
Dramatic Pauses
Everyday Object Lessons
Games (Ideas Library)
Games 2 (Ideas Library)
Games 3 (Ideas Library)
Good Sex: A Whole-Person Approach to Teenage Sexuality and God
Great Fundraising Ideas for Youth Groups
More Great Fundraising Ideas for Youth Groups
Great Retreats for Youth Groups
Holiday Ideas (Ideas Library)
Hot Illustrations for Youth Talks
More Hot Illustrations for Youth Talks
Still More Hot Illustrations for Youth Talks
Ideas Library on CD-ROM
Incredible Questionnaires for Youth Ministry
Junior High Game Nights
More Junior High Game Nights
Kickstarters: 101 Ingenious Intros to Just about Any Bible Lesson
Live the Life! Student Evangelism Training Kit
Memory Makers
The Next Level Leader's Guide
Play It! Over 150 Great Games for Youth Groups
Roaring Lambs
Special Events (Ideas Library)
Spontaneous Melodramas
Spontaneous Melodramas 2
Student Leadership Training Manual
Student Underground: An Event Curriculum on the Persecuted Church
Super Sketches for Youth Ministry
Talking the Walk
Teaching the Bible Creatively
Videos That Teach
What Would Jesus Do? Youth Leader's Kit
Wild Truth Bible Lessons
Wild Truth Bible Lessons 2
Wild Truth Bible Lessons—Pictures of God
Wild Truth Bible Lessons—Pictures of God 2
Worship Services for Youth Groups

PROFESSIONAL RESOURCES

Administration, Publicity, & Fundraising (Ideas Library)
Dynamic Communicators Workshop
Equipped to Serve: Volunteer Youth Worker Training Course
Help! I'm a Junior High Youth Worker!
Help! I'm a Small-Group Leader!
Help! I'm a Sunday School Teacher!
Help! I'm a Volunteer Youth Worker!
How to Expand Your Youth Ministry
How to Speak to Youth...and Keep Them Awake at the Same Time
Junior High Ministry (Updated & Expanded)
The Ministry of Nurture: A Youth Worker's Guide to Discipling Teenagers
Postmodern Youth Ministry
Purpose-Driven® Youth Ministry
Purpose-Driven® Youth Ministry Training Kit
So That's Why I Keep Doing This! 52 Devotional Stories for Youth Workers
A Youth Ministry Crash Course
Youth Ministry Management Tools
The Youth Worker's Handbook to Family Ministry

ACADEMIC RESOURCES

Four Views of Youth Ministry & the Church
Starting Right: Thinking Theologically About Youth Ministry

DISCUSSION STARTERS

Discussion & Lesson Starters (Ideas Library)
Discussion & Lesson Starters 2 (Ideas Library)
EdgeTV
Get 'Em Talking
Keep 'Em Talking!
Good Sex: A Whole-Person Approach to Teenage Sexuality & God
High School TalkSheets—Updated!
More High School TalkSheets—Updated!
High School TalkSheets Psalms and Proverbs—Updated!
Junior High and Middle School TalkSheets—Updated!
More Junior High and Middle School TalkSheets—Updated!
Junior High and Middle School TalkSheets Psalms and Proverbs—Updated!
Real Kids: Short Cuts
Real Kids: The Real Deal—on Friendship, Loneliness, Racism, & Suicide
Real Kids: The Real Deal—on Sexual Choices, Family Matters, & Loss
Real Kids: The Real Deal—on Stressing Out, Addictive Behavior, Great Comebacks, & Violence
Real Kids: Word on the Street
Unfinished Sentences: 450 Tantalizing Statement-Starters to Get Teenagers Talking & Thinking
What If...? 450 Thought-Provoking Questions to Get Teenagers Talking, Laughing, and Thinking
Would You Rather...? 465 Provocative Questions to Get Teenagers Talking
Have You Ever...? 450 Intriguing Questions Guaranteed to Get Teenagers Talking

ART SOURCE CLIP ART

Stark Raving Clip Art (print)
Youth Group Activities (print)
Clip Art Library Version 2.0 CD-ROM

DIGITAL RESOURCES

Clip Art Library Version 2.0 CD-RPOM
Ideas Library on CD-ROM
Youth Ministry Management Tools

VIDEOS AND VIDEO CURRICULUMS

Dynamic Communicators Workshop
EdgeTV
Equipped to Serve: Volunteer Youth Worker Training Course
The Heart of Youth Ministry: A Morning with Mike Yaconelli
Live the Life! Student Evangelism Training Kit
Purpose-Driven® Youth Ministry Training Kit
Real Kids: Short Cuts
Real Kids: The Real Deal—on Friendship, Loneliness, Racism, & Suicide
Real Kids: The Real Deal—on Sexual Choices, Family Matters, & Loss
Real Kids: The Real Deal—on Stressing Out, Addictive Behavior, Great Comebacks, & Violence
Real Kids: Word on the Street
Student Underground: An Event Curriculum on the Persecuted Church
Understanding Your Teenager Video Curriculum
Youth Ministry Outside the Lines: The Dangerous Wonder of Working with Teenagers

STUDENT RESOURCES

Downloading the Bible: A Rough Guide to the New Testament
Downloading the Bible: A Rough Guide to the Old Testament
Grow For It Journal through the Scriptures
So What Am I Gonna Do With My Life? Journaling Workbook for Students
Spiritual Challenge Journal: The Next Level
Teen Devotional Bible
What (Almost) Nobody Will Tell You about Sex
What Would Jesus Do? Spiritual Challenge Journal
Wild Truth Journal for Junior Highers
Wild Truth Journal—Pictures of God
Wild Truth Journal—Pictures of God 2

SO YOU WANNA GET YOUR KIDS TALKING ABOUT REAL-LIFE ISSUES?

Then don't miss the full set of updated TalkSheets!

JUNIOR HIGH • MIDDLE SCHOOL TALKSHEETS—UPDATED!

MORE JUNIOR HIGH • MIDDLE SCHOOL TALKSHEETS—UPDATED!

JUNIOR HIGH • MIDDLE SCHOOL TALKSHEETS PSALMS & PROVERBS—UPDATED!

HIGH SCHOOL TALKSHEETS—UPDATED!

MORE HIGH SCHOOL TALKSHEETS—UPDATED!

HIGH SCHOOL TALKSHEETS PSALMS & PROVERBS—UPDATED!

www.YouthSpecialties.com